ADVANCE PRAISE

"*Rescuing 9-1-1* hits the nail on the head. The author, Randy Sutton, does an amazing job of illustrating the war on our police, the breakdown of the rule of law, and the irreversible mental toll it takes on our heroes behind the badge. He also leaves us with a plan and a path for Rescuing our 9-1-1."

—**Sheriff Mark Lamb**
Sheriff of Pinal County, Arizona
Author of *American Sheriff*

"*Rescuing 9-1-1* delivers a compelling exploration of justice, power, and society's most pressing issues surrounding the safety of today's law enforcement community. With sharp insight and unflinching honesty, this book dives deep into the complexities of social and criminal justice, shedding light on the human stories behind the headlines. A powerful, thought-provoking read that challenges our understanding of fairness, equality, and the pursuit of justice in an imperfect system."

—**Giovanni Rocco**
Retired Law Enforcement Officer;
Author of *Giovanni's Ring:
My Life Inside the Real Sopranos*;
Co-Host of *Inside the Life*,
a podcast produced by The Mob Museum

"Breathtaking and honest. Randy Sutton perfectly details both the history and current events that have resulted in the destruction of the noble profession of policing. Taking to heart the lessons learned can not only help restore our nation's faith in law enforcement but also reignite hope in humanity.

This book paints a clear and detailed roadmap to repair our nation's faith in law enforcement, paving the way for more great men and women in blue. A book for all—from dreamers, to new hires, to veterans, to elected officials and those who love and support them."

—Allyn T. Goodrich

SWAT Officer
Bestselling Author of *October Strong*

"*Rescuing 9-1-1* is not only a riveting portrayal of the evil forces that are actively destroying the safety of Americans but also a playbook on how to overcome the injustices that surround all of us. Lt. Randy Sutton, (Ret.), has given a gift to each of us that can only be realized if we read and act on the important message this book provides."

—Major Travis Yates, PhD

International Law Enforcement Trainer of the Year;
Bestselling Author of *The Courageous Police Leader: A Survival Guide for Combating Cowards, Chaos, & Lies*

RESCUING 9-1-1

THE FIGHT FOR AMERICA'S SAFETY

LT. RANDY SUTTON (RET.)

RESCUING 9-1-1
The Fight for America's Safety

Copyright © 2024 by Randy Sutton. All rights reserved. No part of this publication may be reproduced, distributed, or transmitted in any form or by any means, including photocopying, recording, or other electronic or mechanical methods, without the prior written permission of the publisher, except in the case of brief quotations embodied in critical reviews and certain other noncommercial uses permitted by copyright law.

For permission requests, speaking inquiries, and bulk order purchase options, email **randy@randysuttonspeaks.com**.

3540 W. SAHARA AVE, SUITE 451
LAS VEGAS, NV 89102

rescuing911.org
ISBN: 979-8-9911569-7-4

Co-written with Lori Lynn | LoriLynnEnterprises.com
Edited by Mary Rembert | MaryRembert.com
Proofread by Kathy Haskins | KathyHaskins.com
Designed by Transcendent Publishing | TranscendentPublishing.com
Photography by Tracy Smith

New International Version (NIV), Holy Bible, New International Version®, NIV® Copyright ©1973, 1978, 1984, 2011 by Biblica, Inc.® Used by permission. All rights reserved worldwide.

WARNING
Some sections contain descriptions of actual events and images that are unsuitable for sensitive or young readers. Please proceed with caution.

Printed in the United States of America.

IN VALOR
THERE IS HOPE
—TACITUS

CONTENTS

FOREWORD by Sir Wayne Allyn Root xiii

INTRODUCTION | Where This Road Leads 1
   What Happens When You Call 9-1-1 and No One
      Answers? 3
   Who Is Randy Sutton? 4
   Why Fight for America's Safety? 6

SECTION 1 | The War on Cops 9
   The 15-Second Video That Nearly Destroyed One
      Officer's Life and Career 11
   From Active Policing to "Is It Worth It?" 17
      Hometown Hero or Convicted Felon? —
        Christina Dages Speaks 19
   The Beginning of the Anti-Law-Enforcement Movement . . 21
      The Great Lie of Ferguson 22
      Unchecked Slogans Wreak Havoc 24
   The Root Is Not Systemic Racism 26
   What Does It Mean to Defund the Police? 28

Americans Are Taking Law Enforcement into Their
   Own Hands 31
Victims Are Revictimized When Justice Is Socialized...... 33
Guilty Until Proven Innocent?...................... 33
   Don't Be Too Quick to Judge — *Jamie Borden Speaks*... 36

SECTION 2 | The Sinister Role of Politics and Media .. 41

A Culture of Racism or Heroism? 43
Working Together Against Racism 43
Stories of Heroism You Won't Find in the Mainstream News... 47
True Justice Is Blind............................. 49
Social Justice Redefined.......................... 50
Retirements and Resignations Are on the Rise 52
Record-Breaking Resignations Leave Entire Cities
   Unprotected................................ 56
The Alarming Connection Between "Bail Reform" and
   Increased Homicides.......................... 58
   Death by Broken Criminal Justice System........... 59
   The Revolving Door of "Bail Reform" 60
   Attempts to Correct Bail Reform................. 63
Beware of Trojan Horses 65
   Persecution by Prosecution 70
   Rioters Go Free as Police Are Indicted.............. 72
The Triple D Strategy 73
A Light in the Darkness.......................... 74

SECTION 3 | The Hero Has to Believe in the Quest ... 79

The Intersection of Evil and Destiny 81
Preparation for the Quest. 85
    Hiring Requirements. 86
    Basic Training. 87
    Field Training. 87
The Warrior Spirit. 93
    A Cop's Sense of Mission — *Dave Smith Speaks*. 96
Cops Don't Deal with "Normal" Stuff 97
Suicides Are on the Rise 100
Suicide by Cop 101
    No One Could Have Prepared Me for This —
    Tony Rodarte Speaks 103
The Fallen Blue 105

SECTION 4 | Make America Safe Again 109

Fighting for Reform 111
Exposing Injustice Against Law Enforcement 114
The Wounded Blue 118
Making a Change by Changing the Language 119
    A Rundown Area of Atlanta Gets a Facelift. 121
Recall Efforts Spark Positive Change 122
    Los Angeles DA Barely Survives Recall Effort 123
    Texas Is Waking Up 124
    Smaller Cities Struggle to Keep Up 124

    An Oasis in the Desert 124
    Pulling Back the Curtain on a Movement Based on
        Rhetoric — *Jason Johnson Speaks* 125
    Standardization Is Key to Success 129
    Giving Cops the Tools to Excel at Their Job 131
    Placing Value on Safety 133
    Consistent Medical Compensation for Officers Injured
        in the Line of Duty 134
    Courage Takes Many Forms 135

AFTERWORD | Never Forgotten, Never Alone 139
    From Tragedy to Legacy 141
    The Fight for the Soul of America 145

ACKNOWLEDGMENTS 149

ABOUT THE AUTHOR 151

JOIN THE FIGHT AGAINST INJUSTICE 155

REFERENCES 157

STAY CONNECTED 163

To the memory of my parents, Arthur and Lillian Sutton, without whose love and encouragement, this book never would have become possible.

FOREWORD

As a father, husband, CEO, TV and radio talk-show host, author, and patriot, I travel the country and interact with Americans on every level of society. I have a deep and abiding respect for those who keep this nation safe—namely, our police and military. And I know there are many millions more just like me.

My father served in the United States Navy during World War II. My uncle was a decorated NYC detective, my godfather was a police officer, and my next-door neighbor was a police officer at Yankee Stadium. I loved and admired them all. They were heroes in my eyes. I believe in the "Thin Blue Line." I have blue running through my veins.

I believe that without those who serve and sacrifice for this nation, the United States would not be the most amazing country in world history, ever blessed by God.

That is why I have been so incredibly concerned as I have watched the public safety in our major cities and towns disintegrate—as those who have been elected by the people to protect them have simply turned their backs on our police heroes and allowed criminal behavior to escalate to unimaginable levels.

So when Randy Sutton was telling me about his book, *Rescuing 9-1-1: The Fight for America's Safety,* I was honored to write the foreword. Having authored many bestselling books myself, such as *Trump Rules, The Power of Relentless, The Ultimate Obama Survival Guide, The Murder of the Middle Class,* and my latest, *The Great Patriot Protest & Boycott Book,* I know what goes into writing a book. Knowing Randy and his passion for public service and law enforcement officers' health and safety, I knew I had to participate.

Randy shared the manuscript with me and explained his concept of "a living book." Turns out, he conducted interviews with public safety experts and advocates and shared them on his podcast for a fully immersive experience.

I was truly impressed, not only by the readability of the book, but also by the unique opportunity to see and hear from people who have served on the "front lines" of law enforcement. I found myself absorbing their passion for right versus wrong ... for keeping us safe ... for enforcing the rule of law.

This new approach to book creation is absolutely a novel (excuse the pun) method of bringing a manuscript to life. Because after all, the entire point of writing a book is to share knowledge in such a way that the reader will not just consume the information but also be entertained, creating a memorable experience. To that end, what Randy has created in his "living book" concept is revolutionary.

The importance of *Rescuing 9-1-1* cannot be overstated. The criminal justice system in America is absolutely essential to keeping our society intact. The very fabric of our Republic depends on those who serve in law enforcement. For without laws and those who enforce them, anarchy and chaos reign.

The harsh truth is that in many of our major American cities, that fabric has become torn and damaged and is in danger of a total collapse. We have seen our cities burn in the name of "social justice"—with radical politicians running interference for criminals intent on destruction, instead of standing up for the safety of the taxpayers who actually elected them.

In cities like Seattle, Portland, Chicago, New York, San Francisco, and Los Angeles, fear has caused businesses and citizens to flee. Many law-abiding citizens are now locking themselves in their own homes at night and living like prisoners.

Hundreds of millions of dollars have been poured into elections to put people into office who will carry out the agenda of destroying the criminal justice system from within. Randy Sutton calls them "Trojan horse" district attorneys and politicians because the voters who have been fooled by their rhetoric and deceptive campaigns have put these evil radicals and traitors in control of the "gates of the city."

They then begin to dismantle the criminal justice system from within. Through the misuse of their power and in keeping with a radical agenda devoted to creating a "New Order" (or "Great Reset"), law enforcement officers are neutered and rendered ineffective. Criminals are coddled and rewarded, while cops and innocent citizens are punished.

Rescuing 9-1-1 is, in essence, a call to action for the silent majority to be silent no more. For the people of America's under-siege cities and towns to band together and be heard. For us to join with our friends and neighbors to fight an insidious criminal enemy through participation in our system of government and become activists ourselves.

In other words, to come together to restore the American Dream, to make America great again, to be safe in our homes and in our places of work, play, and worship. And to honor those who serve in our military and law enforcement, supporting them as they selflessly put themselves in harm's way to protect our country, our families, and our way of life.

Much is at stake as we face the challenges ahead. Reading *Rescuing 9-1-1* is the first step to creating a movement to embrace and support the rule of law. To share our love of God, faith, freedom, family, Constitution, and always country (America first, last, and forever). And of course, to stand ready to defend it. To be resolute in the face of mis-information, dis-information, and WMD (weapons of mass distraction). To celebrate America, American exceptionalism, patriotism, and the Thin Blue Line—the men and women who keep us always safe, prosperous, and free.

God bless America and God bless our police.

—Sir Wayne Allyn Root (WAR)

2008 Libertarian Vice Presidential Nominee;
Host of *America's Top Ten Countdown with Wayne Allyn Root* on Real America's Voice TV Network;
Host of *Wayne Allyn Root: Raw & Unfiltered* on Lindell TV Network and USA Radio Network;
Host of the *WAR RAW* Podcast; Best-Selling Author;
Nationally Syndicated Newspaper Columnist, Creators Syndicate

"I BELIEVE"

A Tribute to All Law Enforcement Officers

I am a cop, and I believe. I believe in my badge and all that it stands for—courage, honor, and compassion. Unity and integrity and sacrifice.

I believe in the men and women who stand beside me with gleaming gold and silver worn proudly on their chests. I know of their pain, and I know of their triumphs.

For cruelty and violence is the acid that corrodes our souls, and it is only belief that can shield us from being consumed—belief that our purpose and destinies lie in protecting others.

I believe that cops are warriors. Soldiers, in one sense, because combat is very real and very personal and never far from their reality. But cops are much more. They are the peacemakers, and their courage is tempered with compassion.

A cop knows that each day might be their last. That violence might take them, and they might fall, yet they go on. They go on because of a belief in something greater than themselves. They believe in justice.

Noble words?

You bet they are, and I'm proud to say them.

I'm a cop, and I believe.

To a cop, justice is not a hypothetical theory. Not a concept open to debate. It is real and as visceral as the mournful sound of "Taps" while another uniformed body is laid to rest.

It is something to fight for and, if necessary, to die for.

Yes, I'm a cop, and I believe. I believe that when my career is over, and I no longer shoulder the burdens of my profession, I will look back with pride. Pride in myself in the knowledge that I did my best. Pride in my brothers and sisters for continuing on, and most of all, pride in my badge and for all that it stands for.

I am a cop, and this is what I believe.

—Lt. Randy Sutton (Ret.)

INTRODUCTION

WHERE THIS ROAD LEADS

"For evil men to accomplish their purpose, it is
only necessary that good men do nothing."

—Rev. Charles F. Aked

What Happens When You Call 9-1-1 and No One Answers?

CRASH!

Suddenly, Susan jolts awake. She jumps out of bed and peeks in the kids' room. They're both there, sound asleep. Her husband is away on a business trip. She doesn't know what could have startled her. Then she hears voices coming from downstairs.

Intruders.

She quietly makes her way back to her room to get her phone. Instinctively, she goes into her kids' room, hoping they will stay asleep.

Don't make a sound, she thinks.

As soon as she shuts and locks the door, she dials 9-1-1. She needs help *now*.

As she listens to the ringing, she starts to feel some relief. The cops will come. They will rescue her and her children from the invaders in her home. It will all be all right—*just please answer the phone!* The phone rings for the third time, fourth, fifth … no one answers.

Sheer terror now takes hold of her. *Where are the police? Why isn't anyone answering?* What does she do now?

This story may seem far-fetched, but the stark reality is that situations like this are happening all across America every day … in countless cities … to innocent families.

Our protectors and defenders are disappearing. But it hasn't always been this way.

Among the culture of law enforcement, police officers have traditionally seen themselves as sheepdogs whose job is to protect the innocent sheep from harm.

Unfortunately, these sheepdogs, who are trained to protect the flock, are being accused of being wolves, even though the actual wolves are criminally minded individuals whose intent is to steal, kill, and destroy.

So what happens when the sheepdogs are perceived as the enemy? What happens to the flock?

They are left to defend themselves. Untrained and unprotected.

Moms, dads, children, young adults, babies, grandparents, and the elderly are not trained to face criminal predators in life-threatening situations.

Without the sheepdogs living in proximity to the sheep, constantly patrolling, aware and alert, and always on the lookout for danger, the wolves can easily prey upon the defenseless. They see an easy target and go in for the kill.

No flock is safe without sheepdogs to keep the wolves at bay. And no sheepdog deserves to be treated like a wolf.

Who Is Randy Sutton?

I remember the days when we used to teach our children that if they got lost, they should find a police officer and tell them, "I can't find Mommy."

But in many families, that's not what children are now learning.

We're actually destroying the trust between the police and the people they serve.

Through the rise of political agendas, out-of-context videos on social media, and social movements lacking accountability, our men and women in blue are being painted as villains. Far too many everyday heroes have gone into hiding, fearing for their own safety.

In fact, when I began the journey of writing this book, I almost called it *Heroes in Hiding* because ever since the "Defund the Police" movement started, I've seen countless officers face threats of violence, unspeakable abuse, and unbelievable discrimination.

My name is Randy Sutton, and I was not only a cop for 34 years, but I've also been a police trainer for thousands of other officers all over the country. I had to take early retirement because I suffered a stroke in my patrol car.

Through that horrific experience, which I describe in detail later, I discovered a huge void where there should have been resources. As a result, I created a non-profit organization called The Wounded Blue: The National Assistance and Support Organization for Injured and Disabled Law Enforcement Officers.

Since founding The Wounded Blue, I've become known as the "Voice for American Law Enforcement." You might have seen me on the news recently offering expert commentary or, several years ago, on the television show *COPS*.

When I became a cop back in 1977, I was a 19-year-old kid in Princeton, New Jersey. I was one of the youngest officers in the state. I was kind of an anomaly. I loved musical theater, which didn't exactly make me popular among my peers. I got teased all the time for singing songs from Broadway musicals. I have the heart of an artist and the training of a warrior.

I served for 10 years in Princeton before I joined the Las Vegas metropolitan police, where I served for 24 years, retiring as a lieutenant. I've seen the best of humanity and the worst of humanity, and I'm on a mission to help the best overcome the worst.

My lifetime of experience in and around law enforcement has taught me that unspeakable evil exists in the world. Most people are able to go throughout their entire lives without encountering this level of evil. Cops are called in to face it on a daily basis—sometimes multiple times a day.

Imagine being part of someone's worst day, then someone else's worst day, then someone else's worst day, and then going back to work to do it all over again day after day, week after week, and year after year. This is the sacrifice of our men and women in blue.

Why Fight for America's Safety?

We've seen a massive surge of violence across America for many years now. Our cities are being overrun by crime. From Los Angeles to Portland, Minneapolis to New York City, and Chicago to Baltimore, violent crime only continues to rise.

With the concerted effort of politicians and media campaigns to dehumanize and demean law enforcement, we've seen a decrease in the number of police officers nationwide.

Fewer and fewer new cadets are joining the police force, and more and more seasoned officers are leaving, which means the likelihood increases that dialing 9-1-1 will result in an unanswered call.

When the American people are left to police themselves, our neighborhoods become less safe. That puts the safety of our nation in jeopardy. So I call for unity right now because unless our nation unites behind law enforcement, we will give in to what many with political agendas want—to divide our country and create the opportunity for massive upheaval.

The false narrative being placed in front of America by mainstream media is that there is systemic racism in policing across the nation. As a 34-year police veteran, I can tell you that there are people who wear a badge that shouldn't. There are officers who do harbor racist concepts, but that is on an individual basis. Systemic racism in law enforcement *does not* exist. In fact, we are seeing a more diverse police professional now than at any other time in history.

As a nation, we must band together in a common unity of public safety, of being concerned about each other. I'm talking about the policing world and the concerned citizens of this nation.

I have a message for America—a message that I had the privilege of sharing at the Republican National Convention this year. As the crowd chanted, "Back the Blue," I found myself holding back tears.

We are in an unusual time in our nation's history. We are growing more and more divided, but it's time for unity. It is time for America to stand up and stand together with its law enforcement.

I implore you to read the words on these pages, listen to the interviews on *A Cop's Life*, my podcast, and join the fight for America's safety. Together, we *can* rescue 9-1-1.

SECTION 1

THE WAR ON COPS

"When the sentence for a crime is not quickly carried out, people's hearts are filled with schemes to do wrong."

—Ecclesiastes 8:11, NIV

The 15-Second Video That Nearly Destroyed One Officer's Life and Career

"My heart was pounding," said Christina Dages, wife of Officer Matthew Dages. "It was dark, and there was a crowd of protestors outside our home. We didn't understand why they were there or how they found us."

As she and Matthew tried to figure out what to do, his phone rang. A fellow police officer told Officer Dages that a video from his arrest of Amaurie Johnson that morning had gone viral and was all over the internet.

Since Dages did not follow social media, the officer sent him the clip, and the couple was stunned. One hundred thousand views and rising! How could this be happening?

One 15-second video on social media caused Christina and Matthew to move out of their new home for their safety. The media began an onslaught of publicity against Matthew without having any facts other than he appeared to be a white officer in a confrontation with a black man.

On the day of the event, Officer Dages was on a normal patrol shift. In his role as a La Mesa police officer, he had spent his morning making traffic stops, answering radio calls, and performing his duties as usual. La Mesa isn't a high-crime area, and most of his duties were quality-of-life assignments in a largely affluent suburb of San Diego.

A senior officer had a trainee, so he called Officer Dages to ask if he could help out at Grossmont Transit Center, a trolley station in a part of town where people hang around, sell drugs, and generally make nuisances of themselves. If you don't have a trolley card, you aren't supposed to be in this area.

The trolley station was full of people coming and going. Dages saw a man, later identified as Amaurie Johnson, off to the side of the crowd. He was smoking in a nonsmoking area, so Dages went up to tell him to put out the cigarette.

When questioned, the man first said he lived in the apartments above the station, but after more questioning, he said that he had lied and was waiting for some friends. He started to get agitated, which caused red flags to go off in Dages's head. The man started cursing at him and got irate. A confrontation took place.

Dages asked him to sit down, which he did. Then, Johnson's friends showed up. That's when Johnson stood up and pushed Dages, getting in the officer's face with fists balled. He "bladed" his body, which is a sign of assaultive behavior. As cops, we are taught to recognize this body language as potentially dangerous, so it has to be dealt with. Dages pushed Johnson back down into a sitting position on the bench.

In a matter of moments, the situation went from being slightly confrontational to, "Now you are under arrest." Dages was trying to keep Johnson seated until his partner arrived at the scene, but Johnson was pushing him and avoiding arrest. Dages pushed him back down on the bench, and another officer put handcuffs on Johnson. Dages noticed bystanders hanging around filming him, which he thought was odd. Johnson was arrested, taken to the station, given a citation, and then released.

What Dages didn't realize at the time was that racialized tension surrounding police violence was reaching a boiling point. The George Floyd incident had occurred two days prior, and the effects of it were rippling throughout the country.

"I don't follow social media, so I had no idea what was going on," Dages said. "A fellow officer called me at home that night and told me about the posting. The scary part was that people were putting up my home address, my parents' address, and listing my wife's name. Within about fifteen minutes, I had protestors outside my home and, later, about ten police cars stationed there. It was a huge scene."

Because of the George Floyd event, Black Lives Matter (BLM) and certain organizers had a protest planned for downtown San Diego. When this story went viral, they decided to move it to the nearby town of La Mesa.

That night, riots broke out in the streets of La Mesa. City officials told the cops to stand down as the city burned. The National Guard was called in. Buildings burned, and businesses were destroyed.

Everything changed after those riots. "The tone of the incident changed the environment within the agency. I could feel the tension within the department, and officers were afraid to do their jobs," said Dages.

Incidents like the one between Dages and Johnson happen regularly when police work in a metropolitan area. In normal times, it would not have been anything other than a slight altercation. But because it involved a "white officer" and a "Black man," it attracted national attention. That posting had only a headline with no context of the events that happened.

Dages knew he had a target on his back. "All of a sudden, I was the villain. City leaders and my own police department wanted to get rid of me at all costs."

A few days after the incident, Dages got a call from the city asking him to resign. They offered him a large sum of money—a high six-figure amount—to leave. Dages replied that he wanted them to do the normal internal affairs investigation to clear his name.

"I didn't want their money," he said. "I wanted them to do the internal investigation because I knew I was solid in my actions. I knew I had followed the law 100 percent, and I wanted my name cleared."

What happened next seemed like a scene from a fiction novel and reminded me that everything can be bought for a price. Instead of doing the investigation internally, which is the protocol for every incident that is questioned, the city hired an outside agency—basically a hired gun—and said they wanted them to look into Dages's conduct. They paid an external law firm approximately $100,000 to investigate.

Internal Affairs has a year to conduct an investigation. It usually takes them most of that time to finish their writeup, so Dages expected to wait several months for his name to be cleared. He knew in his heart he did nothing wrong and was simply doing his job.

On New Year's Eve, shortly after the firm started the investigation, Dages was on a weekend camping trip. Surprised by several missed calls from his attorney, he discovered that what normally would have taken almost a year took this firm a mere six weeks.

His attorney shared that there were no allegations of racism, but the firm made up allegations of dishonesty, saying Dages was guilty of falsifying a police report. They accused Dages of lying to them and exaggerating the assault.

"Anyone watching the video would know that was a joke. Johnson was being aggressive. I could have been hurt during the incident," he said.

Finally, the outside agency made a recommendation to terminate Dages. He was fired by then-Police Chief Walt Vasquez. Dages went to trial on a felony charge, and the San Diego District Attorney's office painted him in the vilest way imaginable. The prosecutor had no accountability for misconduct in this matter.

Suddenly, Dages was back on local and national news. All the mainstream media spun the narrative against him and made him look guilty.

"I was still in denial," Dages said. "I thought the DA's office must not have all the evidence, so we gave it all to them, but they still went forward with the case."

The DA, Judy Taschner, had become one of the most progressive DAs in Southern California during the year she was up for re-election. She set out to make Dages the scapegoat for the riots and burnings that took place in La Mesa.

But Matthew and Christina Dages were not going to stay silent anymore. Even though they found themselves caught in the crosshairs of a political war, they were not willing to be the sacrificial lambs for someone else's political gains.

"My wife is a genius and was not going to let me go down without a fight," he said. "She started a Facebook page and began networking and following law enforcement media, websites, and podcasts. She began to get on local news and podcasts to tell my story. I was not allowed to speak, so she had to be my voice."

The Dages family had to come up with funds to pay for their attorney and all the legal fees. They spent over $100,000 themselves and were also able to do some fundraising through social media to raise needed additional funds. Meanwhile, the DA's office put three employees on the case and spent hundreds of thousands of dollars of taxpayers' money, which is unheard of for most trials, including those for murder.

By the end of 2021, Christina was regularly on national news. They were beginning to get some positive social media exposure.

When their case finally went to trial, the courtroom was packed. Officer Matthew Dages sat at the defendant's table. His lawyer set the scene: Dages was a young, intelligent, high-achieving officer with a squeaky-clean record. He and his new bride Christina had just purchased their first home in La Mesa, believing they would stay in his hometown and eventually raise a family.

The District Attorney presented her case to the court over the course of two weeks. Backed with hundreds of thousands of dollars in research and the testimonies of several witnesses, she attempted to paint this officer as guilty. She claimed he had falsified a police report, a felony in the state of California.

During the trial, Amaurie Johnson testified and corroborated the story that Dages told, turning him into an asset for the defendant rather than a help for the prosecution. Ironically, the witness who was called for the prosecution actually became the defense's best witness. An El Cajon jury saw exactly what had taken place, went out for deliberation, and after a two-week-long arduous case, Dages was found *not guilty*.

Later, Dages said, "Every day, the courtroom was packed with friends and family. When the verdict was called, and I was acquitted, you could hear people crying. Special Forces Marines were crying in the audience. It was incredible."

From Active Policing to "Is It Worth It?"

Every time there is the use of force in a situation, an internal investigation is conducted to be sure that the amount of force used was justified.

But the case of Officer Matthew Dages is one of the starkest examples of political misconduct and propaganda I have personally been involved with. Internal Affairs conducted the investigation, and he was cleared of any wrongdoing. The police department determined that he had acted appropriately.

That should have been the end of the story.

But the city burned. They found a scapegoat in Dages and tried to destroy this young man. They made it sound like he was a racist, out-of-control cop. They pushed all this false info out to the media with their spin on it.

What has happened to our criminal justice system where someone is guilty in a court of public opinion until proven innocent? Sadly, this isn't an unusual case. This is happening in multiple states throughout the country.

Dages knew this whole situation was about politics and not about whether or not he did the right thing, so he pursued a higher court to get an appeal. Most cops don't have the resources to fight and are forced to take a plea, but the city just happened to pick the wrong family to bully into a corner.

For years I've worked with law enforcement from all over the country, but not once have I ever heard of a city police department offering an officer money to go away.

Truth prevailed in this case and victory reigned, but not without a long, expensive legal battle.

The war on cops is far more insidious than a physical war. It encompasses a political war where often the same politicians are the lawmakers waging war on the police. It is dramatically affecting the morale of officers across the U.S.

Law enforcement is engaged in several wars at the same time: the political war, the sociological war, and the media war.

Social media has played the most significant role in the future of law enforcement. What is going on in social media now can literally take the life of an officer and create criminality on levels we have never seen before.

Hometown Hero or Convicted Felon?

> *AUTHOR'S NOTE: My co-writer Lori Lynn interviewed Christina Dages for this book in March 2022. Since then, Matthew and Christina have left California, welcomed a new baby into their family, and shifted their battle from getting Matthew reinstated to helping support other law-enforcement families on the front lines of injustice. What follows is an excerpt from that interview.*

Christina Dages Speaks:

The media painted him as a villain, but that couldn't be further from the truth. I know what's in my husband's heart. He's a man of integrity whose mission is to make his hometown of La Mesa a safer place every day.

We have been challenging Matt's termination from the police force, so we are challenging the city of La Mesa. We knew going into this that these cases are hard to win as the strong presumption of correctness goes to the city. We lost the first appeal, but we can and will appeal to the appellate court, where there are three judges.

This situation opened my eyes to the way the legal system is stacked against cops. Matt's use of force was cleared, and even though he was also cleared of the felony, the threshold is low for the city to uphold the termination. Cities use this threat of termination as a tool to steamroll cops to get rid of them for political reasons.

Matt had a slew of evidence in his favor. The city could easily clear him if they wanted to, but they chose to hide behind the legalities. We stood our ground. We wouldn't take their bribe, and now they want to make us pay for it.

We stay in the fight because my husband is a man of integrity. He has been politically crucified for doing his job. The media spun it out of control. No one cared about the truth and facts, so it's important for me to speak up and set the record straight.

It boils down to his character. Because of the person he is as both a police officer and a man, I am proud to stand shoulder to shoulder with him in this fight.

This has been an emotional, mental, and financial battle against an entity that has unlimited resources. We have paid over $100,000 so far, and as we go into the appeals battle, it will be tens of thousands more. We have been blessed to have some agencies behind us, but this would cause many police families to tap out and give up.

This has turned out to be so much bigger than us. As I started posting on social media and reaching out to different agencies around the country for help, I realized how many other officers are in similar situations and don't know what to do.

As I reached out to more and more people, I was connected with Randy through some mutual acquaintances. He was the catalyst that helped us to get some traction in our fight through organizations such as The Wounded Blue. We attended The Survival Summit and got plugged into a law enforcement network of like-minded people. It was incredible.

Again, this is so much bigger than us. We feel we have a higher purpose to help other law enforcement families. We want our story to give other families guidance and hope. It is all for nothing if we don't use it to help others.

—Christina Dages,
wife of Officer Matthew Dages and creator
of @Frontline_First_, formerly @ClearOfficerDages
on Instagram

The Beginning of the Anti-Law-Enforcement Movement

A significant sociological change occurred in our culture in July 2009. Harvard University professor Henry Louis Gates Jr. was arrested at his home after neighbors reported a potential burglary. Gates had returned home from a trip to find his front door jammed shut. He was trying to force it open when police arrived.

The police handled the situation in the way the neighbors would have hoped, conducting a good-faith investigation after a call about a possible break-in. When approached, Gates became belligerent and accused them of being racist. When he became disorderly and took an aggressive posture with the police, he ended up getting himself arrested. The arrest went viral, with a national debate on whether the arrest was a result of racial profiling.

A subtle but very important shift happened when President Barack Obama took a polarizing position, accusing law enforcement of acting "stupidly" by arresting Gates. In his statement, he said, "… the Cambridge police acted stupidly in arresting someone when there was already proof that they were in their own home, and, number three, what I think we know separate and apart from this incident is that there's a long history in this country of African Americans and Latinos being stopped by law enforcement disproportionately."[1]

America looked to its leader, who was critical of law enforcement and demeaning to those who serve. Instead of holding individuals accountable for their actions, our culture at large started to question the entire system.

In February 2012, we had the fiction of Trayvon Martin. Trayvon was killed by a non-white civilian, but somehow the police got tagged with his murder. Even though the event had nothing to do with the police, the opportunists began to see how they could use race as an instrument to move forward with an agenda of racial division, using that incident as a tool to dismantle the criminal justice system.

The Great Lie of Ferguson

To my knowledge, President Obama was the first President to take a position that the police acted "stupidly," and after that we began to see other high-profile leaders take similar positions. The second major milestone in the war against cops took place in August 2014. Michael Brown, an African-American male, was stopped on the street in a suburb of St. Louis after he committed a strong-arm robbery, assaulting and intimidating the clerk at a local convenience store.

When Officer Darren Wilson confronted him, Brown attacked the officer, grabbing his firearm. In the struggle, Officer Wilson shot and killed Michael Brown.

News of the shooting spread rapidly on social media. Rioting and looting erupted overnight in cities throughout the nation. Protests against police brutality followed because of this incident.

A false story took hold in the mainstream media and social media that Brown, a poor, young, gentle giant, was executed by a police officer simply because he was Black. It was alleged that he put his hands up and said, "Hands up, don't shoot."

This false narrative of "Hands Up, Don't Shoot" sparked the myth of white cops systemically hunting down Black men and murdering them. The lies of "Hands Up, Don't Shoot" were embraced by politicians, celebrities, and sports figures. We even had members of Congress stand up—in session—and raise their hands in support of "The Great Lie of Ferguson."

"Hands Up, Don't Shoot" became a slogan for the anti-law-enforcement lobby. This deception, which caught fire in the mainstream media, began appearing everywhere. It still appears to this day, even though it has since been debunked by multiple investigations that were conducted from August 2014 to March 2015.

"Hands Up, Don't Shoot" never happened. The story was made up by Brown's accomplice who was part of the robbery.

When the Obama administration's Justice Department thoroughly investigated this case, they debunked the whole scenario as fabricated, but the die had been cast. It was too late. The seeds from "The Great Lie of Ferguson" took root and a complicit media repeated the claims for months—even though the report was false.

Monuments were erected for this criminal who had just committed a robbery. The President of the United States even sent delegations to celebrate his life—the life of the offender. In truth, *Brown was the catalyst for his own death because of his actions.*

Unchecked Slogans Wreak Havoc

Slogans are powerful—especially slogans like "Hands Up, Don't Shoot" that tug at our heartstrings. Slogans incite compassion or anger, depending on what's lurking under the surface. Slogans based on lies have the power to fuel false narratives and do more harm than good.

Every entity that reviewed the case ruled the shooting incident as justified, but it still created a very dangerous environment for the police because it began the decline of respect for law enforcement.

After the Michael Brown incident, the political redirection, riots, and destruction would die down and then flare up again. The George Floyd incident in Minneapolis, Minnesota, seemed to be the final tipping point.

While various cities saw rioting and looting and arson, the police were told to stand down. Cities across America were burned with few arrests. Law enforcement was basically denied the ability to control the rioting. This led to billions of dollars in damage, deaths, and injuries.

For the first time on a widespread scale, law enforcement was rendered ineffective by the political leadership of those cities. And for the first time in the history of law enforcement in America, people were given free rein by political leadership to burn, loot, and riot without consequences. The movement has continued, picked up speed, and taken on a new slogan: "Black Lives Matter."

These incidents had a domino effect of creating an irrational response to the justifiable use of force by law enforcement. The witch hunt began, perpetuating the narrative that the greatest danger to the Black community is the police.

The ramifications of that continue to this day, when in all reality, the vast majority of the Black community supports its law enforcement and wants them there. The vocal minority, those in the media, and those in political power exploit racial divisions to bolster their own power base instead of showing concern for the safety of the people.

Unchecked slogans like "Hands Up, Don't Shoot" and "Black Lives Matter" are the seeds of insidious rumors that take root and grow out of control. You can't find all the seeds and take them back. They continue to grow and produce their own fruit and make new seeds. The seeds of those lies continue to grow among the anti-law-enforcement lobby, sparking new movements, like "Defund the Police." Politicians, celebrities, and sports figures get pulled in, start embracing them, and promote the new slogans.

The years leading up to 2024 have produced the most detrimental environment for law enforcement I have ever seen—and maybe in our nation's history.

Many states are putting radical anti-law-enforcement legislation in place. This is actually *anti-public safety* because if you take away the power of the police to make arrests or to defend themselves when they are attacked, who suffers besides the police?

The people do.

The Root Is Not Systemic Racism

I'm a realist when it comes to law enforcement ethics. We can list plenty of instances of cops turning bad, going rogue, and crossing into criminality. As long as we have people in power, we will have people who abuse it, whether in politics or policing.

Do misconduct, corruption, and racism exist in law enforcement today? Absolutely. That element has been and always will be around. However, I can also tell you with absolute certainty that no one hates a bad cop more than a good cop does.

Some people will abuse their authority and harbor seeds of racism, but the law enforcement culture itself is not systemically racist.

Racism definitely exists within some individuals and even some organizations. When dealing with people, we are dealing with individual personalities and battling the beliefs they learned from growing up in different areas of the country. That's something we can't hide from. In fact, we need to confront it head-on.

Is this the systemic police racism we have been hearing about in the media for the last several years? Why are we punishing the men, women, and children of America by removing the primary element of safety from their everyday lives?

If a handful of teachers abuse their students, do we villainize teachers and say all teachers are bad? Do we say that kids are better off without them? That's essentially what we've done with law enforcement. If you've ever read *Lord of the Flies*, you know what happens next.

We're already seeing the effects in almost every major city in the country, including Los Angeles, San Francisco, New York City, Portland, Seattle, St. Louis, and Chicago. As public safety diminishes, the strategy to destroy the criminal justice system from within has proven to be very effective.

The criminal justice system is just that—a system. Police are empowered to make arrests. District attorneys prosecute those cases, and judges preside over the courts. If one cog in the system doesn't work, the entire system can be dismantled and destroyed.

In many states, district attorneys have been voted into office with the backing of millions of campaign dollars from such individuals as billionaire George Soros.[2] Soros's strategy has been to donate millions and millions of dollars to fund the campaigns of certain prosecutors who share his political views—Larry Krasner in Philadelphia, Kim Gardner in St. Louis, George Gascón in Los Angeles, Chesa Boudin in San Francisco, and Kim Foxx in Chicago, to name a few.

These prosecutors don't see themselves as prosecutors. Rather, they see themselves as activists who were selected to reduce prosecutions and eliminate incarcerations around the country. They have eroded the criminal justice system from within as they continue to refuse to prosecute a whole range of offenses. Combine non-prosecution with their push for "bail reform," and you have the recipe for de-policing.

The police are out in the community making drug arrests, gun arrests, and robbery arrests, but the DA says they will not prosecute those cases, so the criminals go free. Police officers put their lives on the line every day to make these arrests. If these cases are tossed out by the prosecution, those arrests are a complete waste of time.

Legislation has been passed at both state and federal levels which has resulted in hamstringing the ability of police officers to do their jobs. This has led to a huge increase in violent crimes. For example, the homicide rates in urban centers have risen exponentially, which are predominantly occupied by African American and Hispanic citizens.

This is part of the degradation of law enforcement, one of the most critical pieces of this book. If we are going to Rescue 9-1-1, we have to combat the destruction of the criminal justice system from within.

What Does It Mean to Defund the Police?

People who support defunding the police claim they want to fundamentally change the infrastructure of law enforcement. They hope to limit the existing system's access to money, resources, and weapons. Instead, they want to build up violence-prevention programs, public housing, health care, mental health care, and education.

But that hasn't happened. No plan has come forward to create other resources that could partner with law enforcement. What we've seen is a radical call to abolish the police—not shift resources from law enforcement to other areas, but to completely "reimagine" the entire criminal justice system.

When someone says, "We are going to reimagine the police," what does that mean? It shows such a naive understanding of what a police officer's job is and what they do. Law enforcement is responsible for a broad range of functions, from initiating first aid and mental health support to personal security and protecting people's property.

If you want to get down to the root, law enforcement protects freedom.

People have the freedom to own property, but who is going to protect that property? If you are in California and someone steals your property that costs under $950, they are going free with a ticket or less.

The people who live in big, progressive cities are calling 9-1-1 only to have to wait for hours, or sometimes days, for a response, or they get no response at all due to the record low numbers of police available to dispatch. Even if cops are available, they know the criminal won't be prosecuted, so why bother arresting someone only to have your job threatened? These cities are in utter chaos.

Baltimore is an example of a chaotic city. They have completely surrendered their police. After the riots there in 2014, the police were told to stand down and watch while the city burned. The governor had to bring in the National Guard and police to restore order. Officers were ordered not to put on protective gear, and many were injured. To this day, they have become an ineffective organization because of the prevailing political environment.

The citizens of Baltimore are pleading for their cops to come back. They want the drug dealers gone because open acts of drug dealings are happening on the streets. Drug dealers are not only running the streets, they're also running the city.

The people who live in these communities are asking for help, but because of ineffective leadership, it's a failed city. What makes it a failed city? The desire to choose a political path instead of a protective one.

In a failed city, you might see situations like the one that recently happened in Illinois. A male and female police officer responded to a call about a barking dog left in a vehicle in a Comfort Inn parking lot. The officers found out what room the owner of the vehicle was in, so they knocked on the door to have a conversation about the dog.

The men in the room opened the door and pointed a rifle at the officers. They disarmed the officers, and the male officer was critically shot. They also shot the female officer. The bullet went through one shoulder into the other, disabling both her arms. She ran to the end of the hall, followed by the man who now had her 9 mm pistol. She begged for her life, but the man put the gun under her chin and executed her in the hallway. It was all recorded on her body camera.

These are heinous acts of criminality that our law enforcement officers shouldn't have to face, but the truth is they are facing situations like this every day across the country. They are putting their lives on the line in the name of public safety, but their lives are being increasingly devalued.

This has got to stop.

Americans Are Taking Law Enforcement into Their Own Hands

One of my closest friends is from a rough part of Oakland, California. She still knows a lot of people who live there. Oakland has turned into a war zone. People can no longer leave anything in their cars on the streets.

People are afraid to leave their houses because they know that they could be attacked if they do. If they leave their houses at all, they try to have other people with them.

Oakland is a city under siege. Crime is out of control. If we go to visit friends there, I am always armed. I don't go anywhere without my gun.

With the rise of crime in cities throughout the U.S., 8.4 million people purchased their first firearm in 2020, and an estimated 5.4 million Americans bought guns for the first time in 2021, according to the National Shooting Sports Foundation (NSSF).[3]

Endless stories tell about violent crimes thwarted, not by our law enforcement, but by legal gun owners who have had to take matters into their own hands when faced with life-threatening situations.

An Air Force veteran who served in Iran and Afghanistan, Charise Taylor and her two-year-old son were in their car driving on Interstate 10 in New Orleans on their way to pick up her husband. They got caught in gridlock traffic. While they were idling on the interstate, a man showed up at her window and tried to forcefully open the door.

"He was aggressively trying to get the car door open as he was making eye contact with me," she said. Luckily, she carries a gun, which she picked up and pointed his way, saying, "It's locked and loaded."

The man ran off, and she was not forced to use her weapon.

"You shouldn't have to navigate your own city like a war zone. It's un-American," she said. "Crime is out of control, and it's terrifying. At this point, having to use the same tactics in an American city that soldiers use in Iraq and Afghanistan simply to navigate through the city is scary, and I'm not the only mom feeling this way."[4]

Illinois state senator Kimberly Lightford and her husband, Eric McKennie, saw three masked men stealing their Mercedes-Benz SUV. McKennie had a gun and exchanged gunfire with the thieves.

In Goldsboro, North Carolina, a twelve-year-old boy was forced to protect his grandmother and great-uncle after two masked men broke into their house, shot the grandmother in the leg, and demanded money. The twelve-year-old opened fire and shot one of the intruders, causing them both to flee. That man, Khalil Herring, age nineteen, later died from the gunshot wound. The boy's great-uncle said, "They would have killed us all."[5]

How have we come to this point where twelve-year-old children have to defend their homes against criminals?

Victims Are Revictimized When Justice Is Socialized

In cities across America, criminals who are caught in the act of committing heinous crimes are not prosecuted because their "unfortunate situation" is supposedly "society's fault." In the name of social justice, families are being victimized by the criminals and revictimized by the criminal justice system.

Where is the justice in allowing criminals to go free?

When police are criticized for doing the job they were trained to do, they shy away from proactive policing. In many states, law enforcement officers are not out hunting the bad guys or running warrants. Instead, they're behaving more like firefighters who wait for the calls to come in.

With new "bail reforms," as well as policies and laws that allow criminals to avoid prosecution for certain misdemeanors or even felonies, our officers don't want to get involved or take the initiative—especially when it involves a person of color.

Certain district attorneys are waiting for the slightest provocation to indict police instead of holding individuals responsible for their behavior. Police across our nation are terrified because some district attorneys are now hunting down law enforcement.

"Criminal justice reform" has become the code for turning our criminal justice system into a system of criminal appeasement.

Guilty Until Proven Innocent?

Unfortunately for the good guys, like Officer Matthew Dages, mainstream media is only interested in pushing a political agenda, even if it means steamrolling through and crushing real people's lives in the process.

Not only are police officers prosecuted by their district attorneys, but they are also persecuted through the constant negative narrative spun by the media.

Thousands and thousands of acts of great policing happen every day—acts of compassion, kindness, and heroism. Rarely do we hear about them. But when someone posts a negative fifteen-second video, a city can burn because of it.

Believe me, the media war on cops is very real. Here is a story that happened to me personally:

Quite often, I receive invitations to be a commentator for news channels and other television outlets. After the 2016 Dallas police massacre, CNN contacted me to do an interview about the horrific event. I thought they wanted to hear the truth, and that's why they were reaching out to me.

Before the show, the producer handed me the list of questions they were going to ask me. They wanted to know how I would answer. When they didn't get the answers they were looking for they canceled the interview with me. I never had that happen before.

If you think censorship is not taking place in the media, you are deluding yourself. Now, it is part of the process.

When violent encounters happen, such as use-of-force incidents or shootings by the police, mainstream media often disseminate misinformation and disinformation propaganda against law enforcement.

Facts don't matter anymore. Media is now part of the false narrative. It's no longer about journalistic truth—it's about a political agenda of institutionalized police racism saying that police are hunting down African-American men in order to kill them. This is the story that the political left is pushing. Unfortunately, the mainstream media is on their side.

The outright lies of the media are printed and tweeted and pushed out on a daily basis. A Gallup poll conducted in 2020[6] showed that 27% of U.S. adults polled have "not very much" trust and confidence in the mass media—such as newspapers, TV, and radio—when it comes to reporting the news fully and accurately. Another 33% have no trust at all!

It's interesting that Americans are increasingly seeing bias in the media, but they still believe that an independent media is a significant key to democracy.

In the case of Matthew and Christina Dages, after Matthew was accused of a felony, he was not allowed to speak out for himself. He had to hear and see his name run through the mud, and he couldn't do anything to defend himself.

But Christina could! She played a heroic role in defending her husband's name and in his eventual acquittal on the charges.

"I want to spend my career being a police officer," Officer Dages said. "I want to align myself with leadership I believe in and stand behind as a police officer. I believe that law enforcement needs good leadership, and one day I see myself in a leadership position to help others and to be a voice."

As we close this section, I want to share a perspective with you from an expert consultant in Critical Incident Review. Jamie

Borden has 24 years combined experience in law enforcement, force analysis, video review, and examination. He is highly trained to look at evidence to determine if use of force was warranted.

The next time you hear about law enforcement in the news or watch a viral video, I want to encourage you to try to see through Jamie's lens and ask questions before making assumptions.

Don't Be Too Quick to Judge

Jamie Borden Speaks:

When cops show up to a service call, that's one of ten to fifteen calls they might have made in an eight-to-twelve-hour shift. They are dealing with all the responsibilities that an officer is required to balance during every single call, every single day, with the knowledge that for the person instigating the call, this might be the worst day of their life.

Officers in training are taught officer safety. They need this training to be able to see the threat cues and know what to do in different scenarios. Even then, they can't predict the future. They don't know how the situation will turn out. They have to go into every situation with an elevated level of alertness, a sense of engagement of what's going on in the environment. They have to show up and handle the situation at face value.

Officers are tasked with reading unpredictable scenarios and foreseeing outcomes before they happen. But they aren't superhuman. If they knew beforehand whether or not a person was malevolent, they could make better decisions. But they don't know in the moment, and many incidents are chaotic, tense, and rapidly evolving engagements.

It's hard to balance all of these responsibilities, which creates the potential for mistakes. The question is: Were the mistakes made in good faith? When the use of force is rendered, a scientific approach is in place to determine whether the use of force was justified.

This scientific approach was set by the Supreme Court in 1989. The standard for objective reasonableness uses hindsight as an analytical tool to determine whether use of force was reasonable at the time.

My review and analysis of these cases is very compartmentalized. A specific process and protocol has to be in place to effectively review and analyze these cases. But the human factor also has to be considered to understand human performance before, during, and after the incident.

Take the April 2022 scenario that made the headlines in Grand Rapids, Michigan. According to reports, suspect Patrick Lyoya tried to run away from an officer. A lengthy struggle followed, involving a taser that missed Lyoya twice. The video shows the suspect grabbing for the stun gun while the two were struggling on the ground and the officer telling him repeatedly to let it go. Lyoya doesn't. The officer pulled his gun and fired, killing Lyoya.

Multiple videos of this event immediately went viral, featuring Lyoya's father saying his son was "killed like an animal."[7]

Afterward, protests and riots, calls to arrest the officer, cries for revenge against the officer, and media condemning the officer were all based on one video that had had no time to be analyzed. These knee-jerk reactions were not based on the realities of what happened because nobody knew the actual facts. This is the danger of videos that go viral.

How the video is framed and who controls the narrative can be damaging. Once the narrative has been spun in a biased direction, the damage is done. Everything else reported after the fact will go through a lens by the public where all the efforts at every level of the investigation will be viewed as excuses and abdication for the officer's actions.

This is an incident where I or someone with my expertise would be brought in. When there is a use of force, the videos never look good. People look at all the cop movies on TV and think that a fight can go on for a long time, but in reality, after about a minute of intense struggle between two men, even if they are in good shape, they will be fatigued and gasping for breath.

The video goes viral and we can "see" what happened. It looks like it looks, but that doesn't answer WHY it happened. An important part of an analysis is to get the WHY from the officer's perspective. We get the physical evidence from the scene, interview the officers to find out their knowledge of the situation and their thought process going into the incident, watch all the videos and compile data. We have to understand why the cop's actions made sense to them at that moment.

People analyze the videos as a viewer and make judgments on why it doesn't make sense. It might not make sense to me at first sight, but I am impartial until an analysis is conducted to sort out what the officer was thinking. This is paramount. Were his actions reasonable based on what he was dealing with at that moment?

That doesn't automatically make it justifiable or reasonable, but it is a place to start to dig in. Many technical aspects of this deal with the physiological aspects of the human body and mind such as the cop's focus of attention, fatigue, and unintentional lack of awareness. I am looking for info and data to support the cop's statement, as well as forensic data from the scene. A video is not stand-alone proof of guilt or innocence.

What can we do so we aren't manipulated by the media and the narrative? Ask WHY. As we see headlines and breaking news, we should ask ourselves what we know about this incident. Who is framing the video? Who controls the narrative?

These questions of WHY won't be answered immediately. Analysts need time to determine all the factors. Why did these actions make sense to the cop? What information did they have or not have when they arrived at the scene? All the data needs to be viewed through a scrutinized lens.

Don't get sucked into the sensationalized media hype and take the video or the headline at face value. These headlines are purposefully driven with a political agenda, not on fairness or anything resembling that.

That's not to say that cops don't make mistakes or do the wrong thing. People think I protect the police, but I don't. I protect law enforcement. I can't blindly protect all behavior. If law enforcement officers don't apply themselves as practiced individuals, they are endangering themselves and others. I don't choose one side or the other. I call what I see. Human life is important. Your safety and the safety of those we are protecting is the top rung.

—Jamie Borden,
Founder of CIR (Critical Incident Review)
and Force Investigations Specialist

SECTION 2

THE SINISTER ROLE OF POLITICS AND MEDIA

"When people first come into contact with crime, they abhor it. If they remain in contact with crime for a time, they become accustomed to it, and endure it. If they remain in contact with it long enough, they finally embrace it, and become influenced by it."

—Napoleon Hill

A Culture of Racism or Heroism?

If the American public were exposed to the amazing heroism that goes on day after day by law enforcement officers in this country, they would have a completely different view of those officers.

The media would have you believe otherwise, but in nearly four decades of service, working with police officers all over the country, I have found no culture of racism for law enforcement officers in the U.S. What I have seen, instead, is a culture of heroism.

The vast majority of men and women who decide to put on that badge and take up the job of a law enforcement officer are mainly doing it as a way to give back to their community. They see themselves as protectors. They risk their lives, they risk devastating injury, and they risk psychological trauma around the clock, every single day.

From small gestures of kindness to incredible acts of heroism, police officers help their communities day in and day out, 24 hours a day, 7 days a week, 365 days a year. They never know what their day will be like—they can go from a noise complaint to a gun run to a report of a baby not breathing. They are always ready to answer any call.

Working Together Against Racism

In 1991, I was working in Las Vegas when the Rodney King riots broke out. America had a lot of racial tension, and Rodney

King was a watershed moment for law enforcement that dramatically changed the course of policing forever.

In Las Vegas, the riots hit us just like in Los Angeles and other cities around the country, but the only place in Las Vegas that burned was the part of town on my beat. The Black community set itself on fire and destroyed the only shopping district that existed for them. I wound up on duty for days, and we were in real, no-bullshit combat.

I was a narcotics detective at the time, but I happened to be in an unmarked car downtown when the riots began. I wound up attaching myself to a unit that was on duty during the riots.

One night, while the city was burning, a Caucasian family in our area was besieged by their neighbors. Their home was under attack.

As part of the volunteer unit, I went in to rescue them. We drove right into the ambush in our unmarked police cars. We couldn't see who was shooting at us in the pitch dark, but the bullets were whizzing by and hitting our cars. We were firing back at nothing more than muzzle flashes.

We fought our way to the door, rescued the family, and fought our way out. Our cars were shot to hell. I had never seen anything like it.

For those actions, my fellow officers and I received medals of valor.

The city continued to suffer the fallout from the riot for a long time. For years, no one rebuilt the only commercial shopping area for this predominantly African-American community.

As a squad, this was heartbreaking. The issues of the rioters trickled down to squad level, with tension increasing between some of the Black cops and the white cops. I had to intervene in verbal arguments that developed.

I sat everyone down in a room, and we talked about harsh topics surrounding our feelings and about how some of the Black cops felt that the white cops were showing signs of bias. It was not an easy conversation to have. But by the end of the day, all of us had a much greater understanding—and a much stronger unity.

In policing, you have to be tight. You are either the backup for another officer, or another officer is the backup for you. You may be called upon to save their life, or you may be called upon to take a life for that person. It doesn't get any more personal than that.

The interesting point is that every cop knows prejudice. But when I say prejudice, I don't mean that it's negative or harmful. "Prejudice" is prejudging. And that prejudging can be either positive or negative.

Prejudging situations based on experience is wisdom. Prejudice is different. For example, some people see law enforcement officers as heroic figures who can do no wrong. That's prejudice with a positive connotation.

When we talk about prejudice in the form of bigotry (bias), we must understand that all bias is rooted in intolerance and fear. We naturally fear what we don't know. We can alleviate bias through communication and legitimate interaction. We can overcome fear through proximity. As fear decreases, we become more tolerant.

That's the goal of this book: to reveal that we aren't different. We have our differences, but everyone wants the same thing. Everyone wants to feel secure. We want our families to be safe.

Currently, our country is not headed in that direction, but we can course-correct. When Sir Robert Peel, the "Father of Modern Policing," created the concept of a modern police service in London in the 1800s, he coined a very important phrase:

> **"The Police are the Public; the Public are the Police."**

Never before has this phrase been more poignant than it is today. Our police can't make this country safe without its people standing with them shoulder to shoulder. We can do it, though, if we work together.

One of the first steps is to recognize that much of what is fed to us through mainstream media has a hidden agenda. We need to open our eyes to the lies that are portrayed and propagated in the media and replace them with the truth. And we need to dig for real news about the true acts of heroism that happen every day.

I've collected a few of these stories in the next section. I want to encourage you to share the ones that impact you with your friends and family to help spread real news about true acts of heroism. And if you'd like to hear more remarkable stories about our nation's heroes, tune into my podcast, *A Cop's Life*.

Stories of Heroism You Won't Find in the Mainstream News

While on her routine patrol in Pleasant Hills, Pennsylvania, officer Kristin Mitrisin was flagged down on Route 51 by frantic parents because their nine-day-old baby wasn't breathing. The baby's face was turning blue, so Mitrisin took the baby and immediately began performing CPR, which is a delicate procedure on such a tiny infant.

The baby took a shallow breath, then a few more, and then she started crying. Officer Mitrisin had saved her life.[8]

Trooper Toni Schuck saved an untold number of innocent lives when she intentionally used her patrol car as a shield to stop a speeding drunk driver who was about to run into a crowd of runners on a bridge.

Knowing that she would face serious injury or even death by her actions, Schuck instantly made her decision. The wrong-way driver plowed into her vehicle instead of the thousands attending a 10K race on Skyway Bridge.

Schuck is a hero. Thankfully she lived, but she was seriously injured. Her bravery and sacrifice should be heralded across this nation.[9]

Officer Erika Urrea was patrolling an area near some railroad tracks in Lodi, California, when she saw a man in a wheelchair. As she pulled up in her patrol car, she noticed that he appeared to have his wheelchair stuck on the tracks. Just at that moment, the crossing arms started coming down to announce an oncoming Union Pacific train.

As captured on her body camera video, Urrea jumped from her car and ran toward the man, attempting to pull his chair off the tracks. Seeing that it was wedged in the rails, she grabbed the 66-year-old man, pulled him out of the chair, and they both fell to the ground as the train barreled across the track right in front of them, metal wrenching as the train struck the wheelchair along with the man's leg.

The video showed that this all happened in 15 seconds. The man was injured but was expected to survive thanks to her quick response. "Officer Urrea risked her own life to save another. We are extremely proud of her heroism," said the Lodi Police Department in a Facebook post.[10]

A plane crashed on train tracks around Los Angeles. Officers arrived at the scene. The pilot was stuck in the plane on the tracks, and a train was barreling toward them as the officers risked their lives to get him out of the plane. It was all filmed on their body cameras, and it was heroic.

South Bend officer Ron Glon showed up on a Sunday afternoon to lend his support to twelve-year-old Jaelynn Wilson, who set up a lemonade stand every few weeks in his neighborhood.

Glon helped Wilson set up the stand and worked with him, waiting on people, serving them drinks, and collecting the money. He also told Wilson's grandmother that he would match 100% of the profits.

"I'm out of words. I'm out of words, it's crazy," said young Wilson. "I thought of him as a family member because it really meant a lot for a police officer to help somebody who they don't even know."

Glon wanted to show young kids that the police were there to support them. "His mother was concerned about him not knowing whether or not to trust police officers. My job is to tell him that he has nothing to worry about. Don't be fearful, don't be afraid of us."[11]

Phoenix police officers Rudy Castillo and Joel Kaminsky saved a man trapped in a burning car. Kaminsky first tried to crack the car window as smoke was billowing out, but he couldn't break it. Officer Castillo retrieved a fire extinguisher, smashed the window, and pulled the driver to safety.

"In situations where we don't have time to hesitate, our training kicks in, and that could mean the difference between life and death …" —a tweet from @PhoenixPolice.[12]

True Justice Is Blind

What's terrifying to me—and the main reason I wrote this book—is that we're starting to see officers step back from doing acts of heroism like the examples you just read because of what's been happening to them and how they're being treated by the so-called "justice system."

Traditionally, social justice has been defined as fairness, in spite of race, religion, or culture. We have a strong symbol in the U.S. for social justice. She is Lady Justice—wearing her blindfold and holding her sword and her scales—"blind" to race, religion, sexuality, or land of origin. She holds her people accountable blindfolded because justice is supposed to be unbiased and fair.

Blind justice implies that the defendant should be determined guilty or not guilty with an open mind and without bias or prejudice. Remove that blindfold, and the system that was supposed to be fair becomes open to interpretation. It's the refusal to acknowledge individual accountability without regard to race, religion, sexual orientation, or land of origin. It's the opposite of true justice.

This is what's happening in "woke" cities and counties as the current "social justice" movement continues to spread. "Social justice" has now come to mean almost the exact opposite of the term Americans have held so dear for hundreds of years.

Social Justice Redefined

Fellow officer Dave "Buck Savage" Smith understands the history of policing better than anyone I know. He started his law enforcement career in 1975 with the Tuscon Police Department and became a training officer in 1980, when he started doing national seminars. By 1990, he was the training commander for the state police and took a job with the law enforcement television network, which was kind of like CNN for cops—a 24-hour satellite-based news and training information service. He is now an internationally recognized law enforcement speaker, trainer, and consultant.

During my interview with him in January 2022, he said:

> "When I went through school, Banfield was my guru on sociology and criminology. He wrote that we have to hold the individual accountable. He held society accountable to hold each person accountable. Law enforcement is not just a principle of ruling by

law, but also ruling by a constitution: a constitution rooted in individual values.

"But the opposite is happening now in our society. We are minimizing the individual for the collective, in an attempt to make us a post-constitutional society. There is no longer any concern for the victims of crime in the judicial system. And the fear of going further down this path is that we will lose our ability to have empathy, sympathy, and compassion for a victim. Instead, the criminal will be idolized. We are seeing this happening across America in many cities, and it is damaging the psyche of police officers.

"In many cities around the country, laws have been passed that don't look at the crime but the socio-economic environment of the accused. Criminals are being defined as the victims because of their socio-economic disadvantages. We are hearing the rationale that 'it's really not their fault, it's the fault of society.' Therefore, these individuals are not being held accountable for their actions. So within this new definition of social justice lies the refusal to acknowledge individual accountability. Criminality is somehow a heroic act against the evil empire, and police are suddenly proclaimed as stormtroopers instead of crime fighters."

Our government is advocating for criminal justice reform, police reform, and bail reform. They say they're calling for social justice, but the current interpretation of social justice is completely opposite of what social justice truly is.

What I'm seeing in our modern judicial system is that there is no longer any concern for the true victims of crime. They're not even being mentioned anymore when we're talking about American policing. The victims are becoming nameless and faceless individuals. They're being silenced while the criminals are being treated with the respect that should be given to the victims.

When we lose our ability to have compassion for the victim, and instead we revere the criminal, we not only damage the fabric of society which is made up of families but we also castrate our police force. Imagine going out to fight crime only to have that criminal be treated as a victim because of socioeconomic disadvantages.

Retirements and Resignations Are on the Rise

Officers who are truly competent and good at what they do are leaving the force in droves because of the new norm of policing in America. Early retirements are taking place at an unprecedented rate, and recruitment is down to critical levels. Many of the officers who only have a few years in service are looking at the way things are going and deciding that they don't want to do this for another 20 to 25 years.

A June 2021 survey conducted by the Police Executive Research Forum found a 45 percent increase in the retirement rate and an 18 percent increase in resignations from 2020 to 2021, compared to the year before.[13] This is happening in police departments of all sizes and in many areas around the country. The survey showed that in some of the larger departments with 500 or more officers, the retirement rate increased by nearly 30 percent!

The Sinister Role of Politics and Media   53

When an entire profession is saying, "I'm not doing this anymore," what do the police departments do? They have to lower their standards or close their doors, which is exactly what happened in the village of Westfield, Illinois. That police department has permanently closed its doors.[14] This is not an isolated event but rather a microcosm of what is happening around the country.

The Village of Westfield Police Department posted this on their Facebook page:

> *The Village of Westfield Board of Trustees has made an extremely tough decision to permanently disband the Westfield Police Department. This decision, which has been discussed over the last couple of meetings, was made based on several long-term issues and events as opposed to any immediate quick reactionary decisions.*
>
> *With many of the newly termed "police reform bills" passed by the State of Illinois, it has and will become increasingly more difficult to operate an already financially strained police department at the standards our Village residents deserve. Our agency is currently deficient with needed equipment and we see no feasible roadmap to eliminate the deficiency while at the same time funding new mandatory equipment and equipment needed to operate a police department safely and efficiently.*
>
> *At the same time these decisions were being made officers who worked at the department were also making tough decisions that ultimately ended in resignations from the police department. These resignations were also primarily due to*

> the newly termed "police reform bills" enacted by the State Legislature with such ambiguous questions as to personal liability while lawfully protecting the citizens of Westfield; that coupled with an agency that had difficulty financially supporting the department.
>
> With the new climate in law enforcement, tough decisions such as these presented before the Village Board and Village Police Officers are increasing across the state. Small departments such as Westfield, with limited resources and equipment, are finding it tough to employ certified officers that can perform at levels our residents deserve for what the village can afford to pay ... We want to thank everyone who supported the Westfield Police Department over the years. It has been an honor to serve you!

When entire departments shut down, who suffers? The very people we want to protect.

Many of the officers who are staying are pulling back their efforts. This is what's called "de-policing." When officers don't proactively go out and fight crime, it's as if the department closed altogether. Cops are saying, "You know what? It's not worth it for me to get involved."

In my 34 years as a cop, we used to judge ourselves and our co-workers on the quality of our policing. Are they go-getters? Do they make a lot of car stops and arrests? Do they actively engage in the community?

Internally, we looked at our fellow officers and determined if they were good cops by how effective they were and how hard they worked. The more cars that we stopped for whatever reason, the more people we engaged with. That's how we found the people who were armed, and that's how we found the drugs. That's how we found the fugitives.

We referred to ourselves as urban hunters out to combat criminality.

We called this proactive policing. That's how New York City became the safest big city in the country in the '90s. The cops actively policed.

This process of urban policing is critical to law enforcement. Many people seem to be under the assumption that policing is a reactionary job, that we are waiting for calls to come in like the fire department does.

But in reality, we have to be proactive by going out and looking for the "bad guys," the people who are breaking the law. It's not easy to catch criminals. Now, because of the negative rhetoric about policing in our culture, many departments are waiting for calls, and criminals are running rampant.

This is the most dangerous part of where we are today in America. Our police, our heroes, are going into hiding. They're hiding because they are afraid. Not afraid of the criminals or the physical dangers that are involved, but afraid of the political implications of actually performing policing. We are seeing many district attorneys who refuse to prosecute real criminals, prosecuting the police instead for their alleged perceptions of police misconduct.

Police are being painted with a wide brush of prejudice when they are the ones putting their lives on the line for their communities day after day. Street cops are literally battling crime, but they're constantly worried about the repercussions of doing their job.

The souls of these officers are being crushed in this political environment. When those souls are crushed—the souls of the cops who protect us—we are playing with the lives of everybody they serve.

Record-Breaking Resignations Leave Entire Cities Unprotected

Force Investigations Specialist and Critical Incident Review (CIR) founder Jamie Borden warns that losing a core of our current police force is the "death of wisdom." When I interviewed him for this book in April 2022, he said:

> "Law enforcement is what has given us civility to live a free life in a free country, and that's in danger now.
>
> "New cops have a steeper mountain to climb as the passing of the torch is being snuffed out. They are going to have to turn their own knowledge into wisdom, which takes time.
>
> "People are retiring because they can no longer operate in this environment. With that comes another whole set of problems. We may not see it today, but we'll see it in the coming years."

Even if we turn our system around and hire more officers, that lost wisdom will take years to replace. The damage has been done. This is the end of a generation of wisdom in law enforcement.

When I became a police officer in Las Vegas, there were 5,000 applicants competing for 50 positions. People wanted to be cops. Agencies could be really picky about who they hired. Only one in fifty people could pass the background check. The physical test, psychological test, and polygraph threw out another large percentage. Police agencies wanted the best applicants they could find. They looked for truthfulness, honesty, and integrity.

Ten years ago, if job openings were announced for law enforcement officers in a big city like Los Angeles or San Francisco, you would have droves of people lining up to apply. But recently, St. Louis announced that they were hiring … and *no one* showed up. Not one person. In a major city! In Las Vegas, which hasn't seen as much unrest as many parts of the country, recruiting is down about 57 percent.

Why would people line up to have a chance to become a cop? They probably don't do it for the money. Salaries vary around the country, and while some officers are making a decent salary, the average police officer makes about $50,000 a year. For most, it's a calling. They want to play a positive role in their communities.

Unfortunately, with crime on the rise, cities around the country are struggling to keep up with the crime waves. For example, in May 2022, homicide detectives in Portland, Oregon, were pulled from investigating prior cases to deal with the surge of new cases.[15] Hundreds of families of murder victims will never have hope of solving those cases. Where are the calls for justice for them?

The Alarming Connection Between "Bail Reform" and Increased Homicides

Homicides in Indianapolis reached a new record high in 2021, the same year a young man named Dylan McGinnis was gunned down by a drug dealer with a hefty criminal record.

It all started when twenty-four-year-old Dylan let a girl he knew stay with him. She had a substance abuse problem and wanted to go to Indianapolis to buy drugs from a dealer there. Dylan tried to talk her out of going. When that didn't work, he reached out to her best friend. Her best friend could do nothing to help.

The girl's car was broken down, so Dylan let her take his car, and he went with her so she wouldn't be alone.

They met up with the drug dealer, Travis Lang, to buy Xanax and heroin. Dylan sat in the passenger seat while the drug deal took place. His friend began to argue with Lang over $20, and then she slapped him. Lang got out of his car, pulled out a gun, and fired nine shots into the passenger side of the car where Dylan was sitting. Two of the shots were fatal.[16]

Nikki Sterling, Dylan's mom, said, "I was just at the point in parenting where I felt like I didn't have to worry about Dylan anymore. He was out on his own and an aspiring electrician.

He was a humble guy with a huge heart. Never in a million years would I have thought this would happen. But knowing the kind of person that Dylan was, he would not have wanted his friend to go by herself."

The girl survived, and the whole episode was recorded on her phone. Lang is now in jail for three counts of murder.

What happened next shook Nikki's faith in our justice system. Lang was arrested but got out on bail with the aid of a charitable bail organization called The Bail Project. He had three pending felonies in his criminal history and an existing one. He got bailed out on a $5,000 bond.[17]

"I didn't know anything about these charitable bail organizations, so I started researching them to try to understand how they were able to bail out violent offenders without any accountability," said Nikki. "When I found out more about them, I was shocked."

She found out that they are partially funded by taxpayer dollars in the form of grants from the city. The grants are used to bail out anyone the public defender refers to them. They don't even look at the criminal history of the individual, including any prior felonies.

Death by Broken Criminal Justice System

The taxpayer-funded Indianapolis chapter of The Bail Project made the news when Circle K clerk, Marcus Garvin, was charged with "battery with a deadly weapon and battery causing serious bodily injury" for stabbing a customer at the gas station. Surveillance cameras showed him returning to work afterward, dropping the knife on the counter, and saying, "Damn, that was satisfying."[18]

A conviction would have resulted in his being locked up for a maximum of six years. His bond was set at $30,000, reduced to $1500, and paid by The Bail Project.

This happened three months prior to Dylan's Indianapolis shooting. Less than six months after Garvin was bailed out, he stabbed his thirty-year-old girlfriend Christie Holt to death. After stabbing her fifty-one times, a witness saw Garvin drag her body to a wooded area behind the hotel where he tried to dismember her body.

According to the About section of bailproject.org, "The Bail Project combats mass incarceration by disrupting the money bail system—one person at a time. We restore the presumption of innocence, reunite families, and challenge a system that criminalizes race and poverty. We're on a mission to end cash bail and create a more just, equitable, and humane pretrial system."

On the surface, this sounds like a great cause. Who doesn't want to have a system that is just and equitable? But let's break this down into the reality of what happens.

The Revolving Door of "Bail Reform"

A criminal commits a crime. Then, because of "bail reform" in the name of social justice, that individual is released immediately or given a ticket. But in the past, they would have been arrested and incarcerated.

These changes to bail laws, which went into effect in many states, prevent judges from holding a large range of defendants in jail pre-trial and, very importantly, prevent judges from considering the dangerousness of the suspect in the decision to set bail.

According to the National Institute of Justice, almost 44 percent of criminals released return to jail before the first year out of prison. In 2005, about 68 percent of 405,000 released prisoners were arrested for a new crime within three years, and 77 percent were arrested within five years.[19]

This is called recidivism, which means repeat criminal offenders. Recidivists know how the system works, and they play it. They commit a crime, and then they are processed and released instead of being held. They are free to go out and do it all again, and they do.

This is the revolving door of this failed progressive movement, and the people in these cities are paying the price with incredible spikes in crime. We are no longer protecting the victim. We are doing everything to protect the criminal in the name of social justice reform.

In August 2020, Ramon Luna, a 67-year-old man in New York City, was beaten to death by Eugene Clark, a career criminal. Clark was out on parole for a past robbery when he was charged with assault and arrested. He identified himself on a surveillance video of the crime and admitted he pushed Luna to the ground.

Luna died from his injuries in the hospital, and the Manhattan District Attorney's Office convened a grand jury to indict Clark on murder charges. The prosecutors requested Clark be held without bail, but the judge, April Newbauer, released Clark on his own recognizance.[20]

Two years earlier, that same judge ruled on another case involving a woman who was later charged with murder. In that case, Kaylha Armand pleaded guilty to two assault cases. Prosecutors requested she be sentenced to one to three years in prison, but Judge Newbauer instead ordered Armand to undergo mental health treatment and check in periodically with the court.

In August of that year, Armand was arrested for allegedly stabbing a woman to death.

California instituted a temporary zero-bail policy at the beginning of the Covid pandemic. While it's no longer in place statewide, many counties are still following these policies.

The state's homicide rate went up 31 percent in 2021, a thirteen-year high. According to District Attorney Summer Stephan, "It looks like close to 65 percent were rearrested after being released on zero bail, and of those who were rearrested, 65 percent were also rearrested on a felony crime."[21]

In 2014, a few years before the temporary policies were instituted, Proposition 47, the Safe Neighborhoods and Schools Act, was passed. This law made some nonviolent crimes where the damages do not exceed $950 into misdemeanors. Simple drug possession offenses went from felonies to misdemeanors.

By changing the sentencing for these low-level crimes, this criminal justice reform measure was intended to reduce the prison and jail population. Then, those savings could be allocated to local public safety programs, trauma recovery services for crime survivors, and programs for vulnerable youth.

Was this successful? Across the state of California, smash-and-grab-crime at major retailers has been on the rise, along with smaller businesses as well. The criminals are getting increasingly brazen, entering stores in groups in broad daylight to rob and loot, sometimes running out the door with thousands of dollars in stolen merchandise.[22]

In Saline County, Arkansas, Xavier Littles, who was charged with first-degree murder, got out on a $2,500 bond. He is accused of shooting and killing Teirra Harris at her apartment complex.

In November 2021, Luis Gabriel Ramos was tracked down by an FBI fugitive task force in Salome, Arizona, after he allegedly stabbed a mother and her daughter in their Yonkers apartment. This happened less than a week after he was arrested for arson and released *without* bail.[23]

Attempts to Correct Bail Reform

In Washington State, legislation was passed in 2021 that restricted police officers from using any degree of force unless probable cause existed for arrest or to protect someone from imminent harm. That legislation also prohibited officers from taking someone into involuntary protective custody and transporting them to a hospital for evaluation if they were suffering from a mental health issue. House Bill 1735 restores those powers to officers for both the ability to detain someone based on reasonable suspicion and the ability to take someone into protective custody to have their mental health evaluated.

Another law that was passed in 2021 prohibited police from pursuing vehicles unless they had probable cause that the person had committed a violent offense, was under the influence of alcohol, or a safety risk.

Senate Bill 5919, which was passed early in 2022, lowers the standard to reasonable suspicion.

According to Whitman County Sheriff Brett Myers, the police reforms in 2021 were ambiguous and, therefore, hard to understand. The definitions were so gray that officers had difficulty knowing how to do their jobs. The new legislation gives back many of the powers law enforcement needs to be effective in the communities they serve.

"We had to meet several times a day and say, 'This is what we can still do,'" said Myers. "I think this, [these new laws, Senate Bill 5919 and House Bill 1735] overall, is a win for both the community and law enforcement professionals out there every day doing their job."[24]

Over and over, in state after state, we are seeing repercussions from the bad decisions that have been made when laws and policies were changed to limit the police and the legal system which hindered them from putting criminals in jail and keeping them there.

New York Governor Kathy Hochul is currently proposing changes to the state's 2019 bail reform laws. She said that she feels bail reform has been a success, with fewer suspects being kept behind bars because they can't afford to pay. But she also added that "there has been a distressing increase in shootings and homicides since the law was passed."

She wants to see changes that make it harder for repeat offenders to avoid bail and to allow judges to consider more factors in determining if a defendant should be eligible for bail. She also wants more gun-related crimes to be ineligible for bail.

On Long Island, Judge David McAndrews decided not to follow the bail laws that went into effect on January 1, 2020, in the case of accused two-time bank robber Romell Nellis. Under the law that had just been passed, Nellis's crime didn't qualify as a bondable or bail offense, so Nellis should have been released without bail, regardless of any criminal record.

Judge McAndrews deemed Nellis a "menace to society" and ordered him held on $10,000 cash or $20,000 bond. Nellis had served a seven-year prison sentence and had violated his supervised release at the time of the robberies.

Unfortunately, the judge's ruling was reversed by a higher-level judge, and Nellis was released with an ankle monitor, which he proceeded to cut off before he disappeared. "He's out there, somewhere, able to commit another crime."[25]

Beware of Trojan Horses

Most people don't realize the power held by a District Attorney (or a prosecutor, as it's called in some states). These appointed or elected officials might represent a county, city, or state. They are, in essence, the highest law enforcement officer in their jurisdiction, involved in the prosecution of every criminal case in their jurisdiction. They decide which criminal charges are brought to court and which cases are dismissed.

The website of the American Bar Association, under Functions and Duties of the Prosecutor, Standard 3-1.2, explains their duties:

> The primary duty of the prosecutor is to seek justice within the bounds of the law, not merely to convict. The prosecutor serves the public interest and should

> act with integrity and balanced judgment to increase public safety both by pursuing appropriate criminal charges of appropriate severity, and by exercising discretion to not pursue criminal charges in appropriate circumstances. The prosecutor should seek to protect the innocent and convict the guilty ...

Protect the innocent and convict the guilty, not the other way around.

In many cities around the country, DAs who publicly announce that they are not going to prosecute many crimes are still elected into office. Who is protected now?

They are advocating for a new "progressive" system that they call bail reform and criminal justice reform, which, in reality, means not holding criminals accountable for their crimes.

We have people like George Soros who want to destroy the criminal justice system from within. This is a movement to undermine the very system that keeps Americans safe. They have figured out that if they place hand-picked people into positions of power, such as the role of district attorney, they can accomplish this goal.

Soros has set up nonprofits and other funnel organizations to fund the campaigns of select DAs in large cities throughout the U.S. This network has funded at least $29 million to influence the placement of "progressive" district attorneys. A report published in June 2022 showed 75 progressive prosecutors linked to Soros.[26]

These progressive DAs get voted into office, with about 5 percent of voters actually turning out to vote at an election. Because of public apathy, these "Trojan Horse" DAs have entered the gates invited by the voters who put them into office. They are now given carte blanche to destroy public safety and tear up our system from within.

A prime example is Chesa Boudin, who was elected San Francisco DA in 2019 by the hundreds of thousands of dollars poured into his campaign through Soros-funded organizations. Thankfully, halfway through his term, he suffered a recall, which is a victory for our nation. He was raised by parents who went to jail as convicted terrorists, and he was one of the most radical anti-law-enforcement prosecutors in the U.S.

He was elected on the "criminal justice reform" ticket. Look at San Francisco now. When it comes to the public's safety, the city is a complete failure. Drug users are shooting up in broad daylight on the streets. Children are walking home from school, witnessing disgusting acts and unspeakable evil. Where is the justice for them?

Right now, in cities across America, criminal activity has no accountability. Mass criminality events (like smash and grabs) are commonplace to the point where stores have to put up barbed wire.

These DAs have full autonomy for who they charge and what they charge, and they aren't held accountable for those decisions. The only mechanism to remove a prosecutor for criminal activity is to vote them out when their four-year term is up. Meanwhile, in those four years, they can do all kinds of damage.

They have implemented policies that favor defendants, prohibited prosecutors from filing some misdemeanor charges, and ignored drug laws. Until 2020, most radical prosecutors had continued to prosecute violent felons.

That changed with George Gascón, another Soros-backed District Attorney for Los Angeles County, who faced a recall effort in July 2022. Elected in November 2020, he put into place radical pro-criminal and anti-prosecution policies, which he called his "Special Directives." These policies apply not only to future cases but also to all ongoing and even prior cases.

One such prior case is the release of a convicted double murderer from San Quentin. Howard Jones was approved for parole after serving time for the murder of two teenagers at a party. Under Gascón's reforms, prosecutors were unable to attend his hearing.

These policies, unfortunately, benefit murderers, rapists, cop killers, career felons, and other dangerous criminals, but none of them benefit the victims of these crimes.

His track record precedes him from his term as DA in San Francisco from 2011 to 2019. During his time there, crime skyrocketed.

Before he took office, the area had an average of 151 rapes per year, but from 2014 to 2019, the number of rapes rose to more than 300. Property crime rose 37 percent. The yearly number of aggravated assaults also went up during his tenure, while violent crime in general across the country was going down.[27]

Soros-funded organizations are spending lavishly to elect proponents of so-called "criminal justice reform," but what we're actually seeing is a lack of prosecution, which has led to unprecedented crime waves around the country.

In St. Louis, a suspect approached two police officers in a fully marked police car, pointed a gun at them, and tried to carjack their vehicle. Police wanted to charge the man with first-degree robbery, armed criminal actions, and resisting arrest. However, Kim Gardner, the circuit attorney (their name for the DA) in St. Louis, refused to file charges. Under her leadership, in 2019, the office prosecuted only 1,500 of 7,000 felony charges.[28]

Gardner was later voted out of office.

We are seeing an environment where less than 20 percent of voters turn out. Apathy only adds to the problem. When voters stay home, this kind of situation goes on unhindered. This is the Suicide of America, what I call Americide. By failing to show up, we hand over our power to those who are destroying our city.

In New York City, District Attorney Alvin Bragg, was voted into office in 2022. Within days of being sworn into one of the most powerful prosecutor's offices in the nation, he issued a proclamation that he wasn't going to prosecute for a variety of offenses in order to focus on violent crime.

For instance, he would prosecute an armed robbery as petty larceny. But he said he wouldn't prosecute for resisting arrest, any traffic violation, drug offenses, and prostitution. This put officers in a precarious position where they must prepare for resistance at every arrest.

In addition, he announced that almost every offender would walk free the same day, except for homicides, a class-B violent felony in which a deadly weapon causes serious physical injury, or felony sex offenses. So armed robbers, drug dealers, and felons with guns were allowed to go back out on the streets to commit more crimes.[29]

You might be wondering why the people of New York would vote for someone who seems to be on the side of the criminal. Unfortunately, mainstream media controls the narrative. People listen to it and vote for the people they have been conditioned to believe will work.

Eric Adams was elected mayor in April 2021 on the platform of making New York City safer, but Bragg is openly not prosecuting. How can any positive change take place with this contradiction?

Persecution by Prosecution

If a topic or issue doesn't fit the accepted narrative, you won't see it or hear about it if you only follow mainstream media or don't do your own research. Once the DA is in office and people realize what they are doing, taking action becomes more challenging.

In addition, DAs have the power to review cases involving misconduct or the use of force by police and decide whether charges should be filed.

The city of Portland has a long history of protests and rioting in the streets. After the George Floyd incident in 2020, Portland went out of control with months and months of nightly violence, destruction, and mayhem in the downtown area.

On August 18, 2020, after seventy-five consecutive nights of riots, a small group of Rapid Response Team (RRT) officers was assigned to clear the rioters from the area, so the fire department could extinguish a building that had caught fire after someone from the crowd threw a Molotov cocktail into it.[30]

Officer Corey Budworth was part of the RRT tasked with trying to stop the criminal activity. Two hundred demonstrators, many armed with a variety of weapons, were involved in breaking windows, defacing buildings, and setting dumpsters and buildings on fire. Following their training protocol and in response to the aggression from the crowd, the officers used baton pushes to move the rioters.

Officer Budworth was indicted in 2021 for allegedly assaulting a photographer during this riot. Because of this indictment, all fifty of the Portland Police Bureau's RRT officers resigned.

The Portland Police Association stressed that Budworth did exactly what he was trained to do, and the Portland Police Bureau's own experts found his actions to be within the parameters of his training.

After the internal investigation cleared Budworth, District Attorney Mike Schmidt still went after Budworth instead of the many criminals who were vandalizing the city that night and on repeated nights for months on end. Officer Budworth was caught in a web created by city leaders with agendas from a politicized criminal justice system.

Portland residents will feel the loss of the RRT for a long time. I am intimately aware of this city and its officers, as I spent time undercover during the riots watching the response from the rioters as well as the police.

This is a debacle of law enforcement failure, not because of the police officers but because of the city's leadership. Mike Schmidt failed to prosecute the rioters, but he went after the police officers.

I interact with thousands and thousands of officers all over the country, and I can tell you that these Portland Rapid Response Team officers are some of the best cops I have ever seen. They are highly trained, highly motivated, and dedicated to their city and the people of Portland.

Every single one of those officers had been injured in these riots, and yet they kept going back to defend the public—they are the best of the best. It breaks my heart to see the abuse they have taken from the city and the District Attorney, and the abuse they took every single night at the hands of rioters and protesters.

What an incredible loss. This mass resignation was caused by the failure of the leadership of the police department and the city. This unit's training and expertise will be hard to replace.

Rioters Go Free as Police Are Indicted

In Austin, Texas, elected activist José Garza refuses to prosecute on just about any crime, but he indicted nineteen Austin police officers in February 2022 for defending themselves in riots that were held near Austin Police Headquarters in May 2020, following the George Floyd riots.

Instead of going after the rioters who attacked the police by throwing bottles, rocks, jars of paint, and frozen water bottles, he indicted the officers who used low-lethality ammunition to fight back a crowd of thousands of people.[31]

This appears to be an outrageous effort to punish police officers for following orders and doing their job, while no protestors who became violent with the police were charged. These indictments are strictly political in nature. Garza is ruining the lives and careers of police officers with his radical agenda.

These officers were arrested and charged with criminal offenses. They now have to pay attorneys and fight for their lives and their jobs. They are being charged with crimes for defending themselves while under attack.

What does this show every officer in America? It shows that they shouldn't get involved. This is the chilling effect the anti-law-enforcement movement has on public safety.

The Triple D Strategy

When political leaders create and change laws that negatively impact law enforcement and punish the police, we have a recipe for disaster. Throughout the U.S., cities are embracing a completely anti-law-enforcement ideology.

When I refer to the war on cops, I am talking about the whole picture of the enemies within. The strategy that I am witnessing is what I call the Triple D Strategy:

- Defund
- Demoralize
- Dehumanize

I'm going to add in a fourth: Decriminalize everything. If you decriminalize theft, you get stores like Walgreens, Target, and Amazon closing or moving locations and employees.

Amazon moved 1,800 workers from one of its facilities in downtown Seattle because of the violent crime escalating in the city—multiple shootings, assaults, and carjackings—after the city council approved a budget in December 2021 that cut police funding by more than $7 million. Several other businesses have closed or moved from the downtown area as well.[32]

What happened to leaders who express concern over the true issues of public safety? What happened to holding criminals accountable? The leadership in cities like Seattle seem to be tone-deaf and blind to skyrocketing crime.

A Light in the Darkness

In the midst of all the darkness and chaos, sometimes I get messages that lift my soul. One such message came from a woman named Diane. She has taken it upon herself to start knitting and crocheting Thin Blue Line blankets and giving them to officers who have been injured in the line of duty. She started a nonprofit called Covering the Blue, and now has volunteers from all over the country who help her.

She sent me an email about Heather Betz, one of the wounded officers who received a blanket. It said, "I wanted to share Heather's letter with you because she has included The Wounded Blue in this letter. I'm so thankful you were there that day to reach out to her and that her life was saved. Over the last few days, I've gotten 77 new members who crochet and knit. So, I'm praying they will be a huge help to get more covers to injured officers."

This is Heather Betz's letter:

> I've been asked to share what Covering the Blue means to me, and I'm going to do my best to put it on paper. Let's just say, Covering the Blue helped save my life.
>
> On November 22, 2018, on Thanksgiving morning, I was dispatched to a horrific call. During the call, I was shot in the right eye and face and then immediately lost my eyesight. My department completely turned their backs on me, and I felt alone, in the darkest place I've ever been. I felt like no one cared about me and my sacrifice. I was about to throw in the towel and give up.
>
> Right before Christmas, I received a box, and I had no idea who it was from. When I opened the box, I found a handmade, knitted, thin-blue-line blanket, and a card from Diane Baughman, the founder of Covering the Blue.
>
> The card was a simple one, thanked me for my sacrifice, and told me that she cared about me and was there for me and gave me a phone number and a Facebook page so I could connect with her if I wanted to.
>
> I was extremely hesitant to contact her at first, thinking she really wouldn't care either. Two days later, I finally decided to reach out. I talked for a long time, explained everything going on in my current mindset.

Diane from Covering the Blue could have just hung up the phone and forgot all about me, but she didn't. Within hours of talking to her, I received a call from a group called The Wounded Blue.

They told me Diane had immediately reached out to them and told them about me and my struggles. Because of that one phone call Diane made to The Wounded Blue, she saved my life.

I use my special blanket now every time I'm struggling. I have brought it to all my surgeries I've had since I was shot. It's like a comfort to me. Not just to keep me warm, but to help encourage me to continue fighting.

Since my incident, I've had to medically retire. To this day, I continue to be denied and fight for full benefits from South Carolina, as well as continuing to fight for disability benefits from Social Security.

Every time I feel frustrated and down, I curl up with my blanket and keep fighting, just like Diane does for all her wounded officers every day.

I've had people say it's a nice blanket, but I know it means so much more to me. Diane fights so hard for wounded police officers every day and does everything in her power to make sure no officer is left behind.

—Heather Betz

Finding out that this small act of service helped save her life reminded me yet again why we do what we do. Stories like these give me renewed hope to keep going. Because I also know that Heather is one of many.

When Diane sends the blankets out, she sends a letter from The Wounded Blue with it. She contacts us when somebody's really struggling, and we reach out to them.

If you'd like to donate to Covering the Blue or volunteer to crochet Thin Blue Line blankets, go to CoveringTheBlue.org.

SECTION 3

THE HERO HAS TO BELIEVE IN THE QUEST

"Officers are heroes on a quest. They're out hunting evil. And the hero has to believe in that quest—because every day they find themselves waist-deep in the banality of evil."

—Dave "Buck Savage" Smith

The Intersection of Evil and Destiny

The four-year-old compact car was stopped at a traffic light. The neon lights from the casinos flashed their staccato rhythm and reflected on the faces of the family in the cool Las Vegas night.

Times were getting better for the young couple. Steady work, a small home, and the addition of their one-month-old baby girl, now happily burbling in her infant seat, gave this immigrant family hope that the American Dream might just become a reality.

They were on their way to the store to pick up some formula and diapers as the new father glanced over to see his young wife reaching back to stroke her sweet baby's face with the back of her hand. He smiled as he turned his concentration back to driving and was just about to ease down on the accelerator in anticipation of the light turning green.

They didn't pay any attention to the lowered, primer-gray Buick idling next to them. The shaved heads of the two men inside glistened with sweat even though the March temperature in Las Vegas had people donning their coats. The cocaine surging through their systems had raised their body temperatures and lowered their ability to think or feel.

There was no reason for them to do what they did next. They shared the same ethnic heritage as the young couple in the car beside them, but certainly not their values, not their hope.

Maybe that was why they chose that moment to raise their nine-millimeter, semi-automatic pistols and empty the guns into the car next to them. The bullets tore into the glass and metal, devastating everything in their path.

The baby who, moments before, had been innocently waving her little arms in the air, enveloped in the warmth and love of parents who adored her, now lay almost motionless. She was still strapped into her seat, blood pouring from the horrible gash the bullet had ripped into her face. The mother screamed, and the father punched the gas pedal in a frantic attempt to escape the series of shots fired in rapid succession while shards of glass imploded into the car.

Without a glance back, the two gang punks sped off, laughing, proud of the courage it took to indiscriminately open fire on the innocent.

My patrol car glided through the night on a collision course with this family's destiny. I had more than twenty years of experience behind the badge, but this was a night I would never forget.

I was first alerted that something was wrong when I approached the intersection and saw the compact car parked at a weird angle. I noticed the panicked, jerky movements of the people surrounding it before I heard the woman screaming.

As I got out of my unit, I heard someone yell, "My God, my God, the baby's been shot!" Then I saw the baby seat on the sidewalk next to the car. My flashlight illuminated the tiny face awash with blood, and my heart fell as I saw the little body jerking spasmodically.

I was all alone on this call. I needed three heads and ten hands. Who shot her? Were they still around? I needed to get medical attention for the baby. People were screaming and crying. All I could think was, I must help this baby.

The procedure was clear: summon the paramedics and begin the investigation. But as I radioed for help, I kneeled beside her and found that she wasn't breathing. Then, as if in answer to a prayer, another patrol car pulled up.

It was all instinct then—I didn't think about procedures—I just snatched up the little limp and bloody bundle, jumped into the front seat, and shouted at the startled young cop to get to the hospital.

As I cradled the infant in my arms, I saw that the bullet had inflicted so much damage to her tiny face that she was choking on her own blood and tissue. I scooped out the gory mass with my fingers and then began mouth-to-mouth resuscitation, knowing that the baby had no chance otherwise. I sealed my mouth over her devastated mouth and nose and began to breathe my life into her little lungs.

I prayed between breaths, Please, little one ... please live.

The young cop next to me drove like he was a NASCAR pro. Without a moment's hesitation, he joined me on my mission to save the life of this tiny child. We hurtled through dark alleys and down neon-lit boulevards as the siren pulsed and the flashing reds and blues reflected off the buildings.

I continued to breathe into the baby's lungs, and moments (or was it a lifetime?) later, I heard the most beautiful sound in the world ... she was crying. I had coaxed her back from the edge of no return.

As I tasted her blood on my lips, I held back my tears. In any other circumstance, I would have been repelled by this gory intimacy, but at this moment, I just felt an incredible surge of blessed joy. She had come back to me. As I held this child and urged her to stay with me through my whispered words, my silent pleas to God, I felt an inseparable bond begin to form. My life and that of this tiny little girl had crossed and meshed in some prophetic way.

The trauma team was waiting at the hospital, and I handed off my charge to those who would now shoulder the responsibility for her life. They hustled her away, and I felt my heart pounding beneath my bullet-resistant vest. I tasted my tears before I even knew that I was crying. I prayed as I silently watched them work their magic.

Maybe those prayers were heard and answered because as I looked up and saw the trauma team nurse approaching me, she was smiling. She said that the little girl would be just fine.

She would need extensive cosmetic surgery in the future to hide the terrible scars that would be a constant reminder of this nightmare come true. I gave her one last look as the team huddled over her in the stark light. The reality of the tragedy would never be more clear.

As I walked out of the treatment area, I heard an accented voice say, "That's him, that's the one." I turned and saw the young couple whose nightmare I had shared. They ran toward me, tears streaming down their faces, and thanked me in two different languages for saving their baby.

It was at that moment I learned that the baby's name was Jackie. I had no words. I could only silently wrap my arms around both of her parents. The mother looked up at me and, seeing her daughter's blood on my face, reached up and touched it—almost wondrously—with the tips of her fingers.

I will never know what thoughts ran through her mind at that moment. I only know that as her fingers drifted away, her tears ran silently down her cheeks. I could feel my eyes start to burn, so I turned and walked out of the hospital, back into the cool Las Vegas night, and back to work.

Years later, I was honored to escort Jackie, who I treat as my goddaughter, to her quinceañera.

Nothing can prepare you for life-or-death moments.

Preparation for the Quest

We all recognize heroics in the military. Military personnel train and train for a mission, and they go on that mission. Afterward, they regroup and come home to train for the next assignment. But in the police world, after officers go through extensive training, they go on mission after mission after mission, day in and day out.

Law enforcement doesn't get a break. They don't come home for R&R. They hit the streets every day. If they are working twelve-hour shifts, they are away from home for fourteen to sixteen hours at a time. They go from call to call to call. If we look at the total violence—the gunshots, stabbings, and assaults—policing is more dangerous than ever before.

Why would someone subject themselves to that level of stress? They believe in the quest. They believe that good will triumph over evil. They want to be part of something greater than themselves—to protect the communities where they and their friends and families live.

Before our heroes get into law enforcement, they have to go through an extensive qualifying process that is far more than simple recruitment. Although this hiring process has no standardization within our nation, every state follows several key elements.

Hiring Requirements

Law enforcement officers must have certain personal qualities in order to be considered as a candidate.[33] They have to be intelligent, team players, and quick learners. When people think about what a police officer's job entails, they rarely consider that it is a highly intellectual career. Cops have to engage every part of their intellect to solve situations they encounter and bring positivity to these interactions.

They also have to be medically and physically fit and pass psychological screenings to be sure they can handle the stress that comes with the job. Some states even require a polygraph test.

Next comes a written exam and an oral board interview. A very important part of the whole process is an extensive background check. They have to have a clean record. That doesn't just mean no criminal record. It also includes not having any of the following: drug use, bad credit history, a history of domestic violence, a poor driving record, a poor employment record, or gang affiliations.

This check can take months to complete. The hiring authority will interview the prospect's friends and family, delve into their credit history, and go through their high school and college transcripts. They might even interview teachers or former classmates. It is so stringent that more officers fail this background check than in any other area.

Basic Training

Once an officer is hired, they go through 600 to 1,200 hours of basic training to become a certified police officer. The amount of time and the requirements vary from state to state, but every person has to pass all the areas of competency. This includes firearm proficiency, defensive tactics, criminal law, and de-escalation training, among many others. Every avenue of proficiency has to be demonstrated, along with physical fitness.

Law enforcement is not getting the kind of training that we think they do. Even before "defunding," training was scarce because of the time involved, manning issues, and finding the funding.

With the current trend to defund the police, more money is being taken away from these departments, and cops aren't getting access to the information they need to help them make good decisions.

Field Training

In field training, rookie officers are paired up with field training officers (FTO) who have specialized skills to train new recruits.

This is where new officers learn to apply their academy training to the streets. This is always a uniform job in a patrol division.

During this time, which is usually around six months, these officers are evaluated every single day to see if they can cut it in the real world of policing. They learn the job of policing on the streets. They are trained in the basic skills necessary to be on their own as a one-officer unit.

A large part of my career was focused on field training. I started out as an FTO, then later was promoted to Field Training Sergeant. I was a Field Training Lieutenant when I retired. Over the years, I evaluated hundreds of officers and molded them into safe and effective law enforcement officers. As a Field Training Sergeant and Lieutenant, I supervised the field training squad—the field training officers and trainees.

An officer can go through the police academy and be a rockstar but still fail out on the street. The reality of policing is far different than the training.

One story is ingrained in my memory from my days as a field training officer. I had a recruit who was stellar. He sailed through the training program. I was his sixth and last FTO before he finished the training. He was a mature guy, a pastor, who knew how to communicate well with people and was a pleasure to be around.

Toward the end of our patrol, we got a call for a robbery in progress about a block away. About a minute later, we arrived at a retail store. A clerk had been closing up the store next door to the one being robbed and saw a guy go into the building with a stocking over his face and a machine gun in his hand. He called 9-1-1.

When we got there, the robber was inside with the store clerks. We peered around the columns outside the building, scoping out the situation to assess our next move. The guy comes running out, gun in one hand and a bag of money in the other.

My first inclination was to shoot him, as he was brandishing his gun. But instead, I yelled out, "Police! Drop your gun." It was the right call, as he couldn't get that gun out of his hand fast enough!

We handcuffed him, and I left my trainee with him while I went inside to see if the store personnel were ok. I came back out, and my trainee had the shotgun barrel pressed tightly against the guy's forehead. He was in a meltdown, yelling, "Don't make me use this shotgun!" He was sweating and out of control.

He realized that night that he couldn't do it. He was an amazing guy, but that situation was too much for him. He handed me his badge the next day.

That is why field training is critical. The reality of the job is that you don't know how you will react until you are put in one of these situations. These FTOs are unsung heroes. They take an officer without any skill and make them into a cop. Their job is to mold these people—it could be hundreds of officers over the course of their careers—into responsible police officers. They are entrusted with the life of that officer and the citizens they encounter.

Each of these encounters leaves a legacy for the entire career of that officer. How that FTO conducts themselves and the experience they create for the new recruit will affect that officer for the rest of their lives.

Society and the media have villainized a key component of an officer's training: the "use of force."

For most people, this phrase might conjure up an image of violence between a suspect and a police officer. But "use of force" in any given situation is not just an action; it is a protocol that officers learn in their training.

Anyone who hasn't been in law enforcement would find it very hard to imagine the complexities of the job. An officer must have the bedside manner of a doctor, the critical thinking skills of an investigator, the knowledge of a lawyer, the reflexes of an athlete, and the courage of a warrior.

Officers go on multiple calls every single day, day in and day out, thousands of them a year. Each time, scenarios will run through their mind before they arrive at a call. When they do arrive, they have to be both mentally and physically prepared for the unexpected. If something is amiss, bells and whistles will go off in their head. They'll have to think fast and act faster. They have to figure out how they are going to handle the situation, and they need tools to help them stay in control of it.

They have a split second to make a life-and-death decision, and sometimes, even if they are trained for it, they are not mentally prepared to do it. That's why cops sometimes die instead of using deadly force at the appropriate moment.

At that moment of decision—some call it "facing the dragon"—they face the fear of not reacting, not the fear of action. They think they are going to do what they are trained to do, but killing someone is against human nature. If an officer has been properly brought up with morals and a sense of right and wrong, taking a life goes against everything ingrained in them.

As an FTO, preparing men and women to kill was part of my job—to be prepared to kill. That is a tall order, and it was also my responsibility to determine who wouldn't be able to do it. In most instances, the officer themself makes that determination and realizes they should not be a police officer.

I am constantly involved in reviewing police conflict videos where the police lost control because they did not use the justifiable amount of force at the appropriate time. This is what kills cops. In essence, if they don't control a suspect quickly and efficiently, they can end up in a fatal confrontation with that suspect.

All law enforcement agencies have policies that guide their use of force. These policies describe an escalating series of actions an officer might take to resolve a situation. This continuum has many levels. In their training, officers learn to respond with a level of force appropriate to the situation at hand, acknowledging that the officer might move from one part of the continuum to another in a matter of seconds. These levels of force protect them, the suspects they are trying to apprehend, and the community they serve.

This full spectrum of use of force is the most misunderstood aspect of policing and the area that generated all the upheaval and put the police in the "line of fire" on social media and in the news.

Let's look at an example that took place in Baltimore. An officer made a car stop to apprehend a man who was wanted by the police. The suspect resisted, and the officer hesitated. The suspect smashed the officer's head against the car, and he sustained critical head injuries.

The officer was legally justified to use deadly force to protect his own life, but when questioned later, he said he didn't because he was afraid he would be prosecuted. The suspect went free, and the officer became disabled.

This is just one of many examples of these situations.

According to FBI statistics, approximately 79,000 law enforcement officers were physically assaulted last year in the line of duty, up from 60,000 three years prior. The number includes incidents ranging from physical pushing to being shot, and this number has been increasing over the past seven years.

The common denominator for 99 percent of all instances of the use of force is resisting arrest. When a suspect is violently resisting arrest, an officer cannot afford to lose the battle. If they lose the battle, they lose their life. If they fail to use the appropriate amount of force at the appropriate time, we might all lose. The officer might lose their life, the suspect gets away to commit another crime, and the community is not safe.

The use of force never "looks good" when an officer has to go hands-on with an individual who is resisting arrest. Defensive tactics are, on their face, ugly. But the officers are doing what they are trained to do to gain control as quickly as possible, which mitigates the risk to them, the suspect, and the public. That's their job.

When the news states that the suspect was "unarmed," that is never the situation. That unarmed suspect could be physically superior to the officer they are resisting. They have fists that can be used to beat, heads to butt, feet to kick, or they can pick up a spontaneous weapon instantly. That officer can't afford to lose because a deadly weapon is in that fight—the officer's gun.

A weapon is always involved because the officer is always armed. If the officer is disarmed during the physical confrontation, that weapon can be used against them. Hundreds of officers have been killed with their own weapons.

The Warrior Spirit

Laws exist to protect people within the norms of their society. If laws are no longer respected nor enforced, society crumbles. If that happens, a new type of society called socialism takes its place, a system that has failed in every country where it has been tried.[34]

Taking credibility away from the police and painting law enforcement as a systemically racist profession diminishes the officers within that system. Are there cops who are racist? Of course, but they are few and far between. And they are held accountable if they use excessive force.

The symbolism of a law enforcement officer is critical if they are to accomplish their mission. You should be afraid to physically assault a police officer, you should be afraid to commit a crime, and you should be afraid of the consequences. Not vice-versa.

When we diminish the police, we diminish society because the police are the most visible part of our government.

Under what's referred to as "21st Century Policing," two critical terms came into conflict: the Warrior Spirit and the Guardian Spirit.

What's the difference? The warrior spirit, which has been ingrained into policing by legitimate police trainers for years. It doesn't mean an officer is constantly at war, but when the situation dictates, that warrior spirit will help them survive.

That warrior spirit is essential. I was once in a toe-to-toe gunfight with a criminal—guns blazing at each other at close range in a life-or-death situation. If I didn't know within myself that I could and would fight to the death as a warrior should, I believe I would have died that night, but the warrior spirit was alive within me.

The warrior mindset for police officers is essential for them to accomplish their mission and survive a career in policing. If a cop is told, "No, you're not a warrior because a warrior is evil," they lose that component of their survival.

During the riots in Ferguson, armored personnel carriers were brought in to assist in handling the riots. These military vehicles had been obtained for police use by the Federal 1033 Program, which allowed the Department of Defense to give state, local, and federal law enforcement agencies military hardware, including armored vehicles.[35]

While it offers the sharing of life-saving equipment a lot of departments can't afford to buy, this has been falsely referred to as "the militarization of the police" and highly criticized by the media.

This program ended during the Obama administration, was brought back by Trump, and retracted again by Biden. What does retracting their use tell our police? It tells them that their lives don't matter. When this valuable tool is taken away—a tool that isn't needed often but can be critical when it is—officers suffer unspeakable injuries and potential loss of life. These vehicles have saved countless lives during floods, natural disasters, and shooting rampages.

Remember the horrific shooting at the Pulse gay bar in Orlando, Florida? An active shooter's rampage ended when the police crashed through the wall with an armored personnel carrier. If they hadn't had this ability, more people would have died.

Situations often happen around the country where SWAT teams face a standoff with an armed shooter in a building with a wide range of fire. Without an armored personnel carrier, anyone who enters that area faces a killing machine.

This has been a topic of debate since the original decision to end the program. Most departments can't afford to buy this life-saving equipment on their own, which creates a dangerous environment for the police when they encounter these situations.

The narrative was that the police were bringing military vehicles in to handle a civil issue. As a result, this life-saving equipment was taken away from law enforcement, creating even more dangerous environments.

Describing the use of these tools as "the militarization of the police" also resulted in diminished police training. Several training sessions on law enforcement survival tactics were outlawed in certain cities. Cops need these skills to survive on the streets. Taking these survival skills away kills cops and diminishes the respect for the lives of our officers, which is what we are seeing across the country today.

A Cop's Sense of Mission

> *AUTHOR'S NOTE: When I interviewed Dave "Buck Savage" Smith in January 2022 about the history of policing, he shared a compelling story with me that I knew I needed to include in this book. Even though this encounter happened almost fifty years ago, he still remembers it in vivid detail.*

Dave Smith Speaks:

Every cop starts out with that same sense of mission. And I was no exception. I was a young man, fresh out of college. I was idealistic, and still percolating in my mind were all these theories I had learned about criminality.

But then reality hit. I can remember it like it was yesterday: that very first rape victim call.

It happened right off a college campus. The victim had come home late and opened the window because it was warm and the air conditioning wasn't working very well in her apartment.

A guy crept in the window with a knife, held it to her throat, raped her, and ran away.

I walked through that door, fresh out of the academy. I can tell you now, you could have given me 100 classes on how to deal with a rape victim, but the actual situation was the most powerful, experiential learning moment of my life.

She was trembling, weeping, and falling to pieces. I thought the last thing she would want to see was a man, but we didn't have any women on my shift.

The lab techs came to the scene to get her ready to go to the hospital, and she wouldn't let me out of her sight. And that's when I realized—she doesn't need a man, she doesn't need a woman—she needs a police officer. She needs someone to be there right now, someone to help her feel safe.

She knew she was calling a person who could bring comfort and safety. And maybe the beginning of hope, the first catalyst for helping on her journey to healing.

I knew at that moment that this was why I was born, to be there and to do this job. I thought, "This is my mission." And I felt it in the deepest part of my soul.

—Dave Smith,
author and creator of JD "Buck" Savage

Cops Don't Deal with "Normal" Stuff

Every cop is drawn to the heroic. They love the quest. But, as Dr. Kevin Gilmartin describes in the book *Emotional Survival for Law Enforcement*, they are the unrequited lover. They love what they're doing. They love the concept of policing. They love their department. When a cop gets screwed over for political purposes, it affects everything they do and who they are as a human being. It breaks their spirit.

As author Dave Smith says, "They love what they do, and they love their agency, but that love isn't returned. That's why you find so many cynical, hard cops with the victim-based mentality Dr. Gilmartin talks about. Their spirit breaks, and they retire on duty. Now, you have a whole nation of cops who have essentially retired on duty, RODs, as we call them."

The breakdown of mental and emotional health is one of the most important issues facing our officers today. Dr. Kevin Gilmartin's Emotional Survival handbook has probably saved more lives, marriages, and careers than all classes and seminars put together. It is the Bible for police officers and should be required reading for every cop.

Gilmartin is a brilliant instructor who talks about how people don't call cops for "normal" stuff. They're called to address the "maddest, baddest, and saddest" issues—the situations most people can't handle on their own. That's why they call the cops.

For example, cops routinely go on "check the welfare calls," which they absolutely dread. These seemingly routine calls have turned out to be some of the most hideous situations you can imagine.

In Brentwood, Tennessee, a concerned grandmother called 9-1-1 to "check the welfare" of her son-in-law. She said she was afraid he was suicidal and just wanted someone to check on her daughter's family.

What the officers found was not what anyone could have expected. The son-in-law was nowhere to be found, but the two-year-old granddaughter was left alone upstairs in her crib.

Dr. Rachel Maidens, the daughter of the woman who called the police, had been wrapped in blankets, shot to death by her husband, and left in the living room behind the couch.

On the kitchen counter was a note expressing regret for what happened and asking for custody of the child to go to Dr. Maidens's mother. The shotgun was by the couch, and the car trunk stuffed with $87,200. When officers came to the home to perform a welfare check, his young daughter said, "Daddy gone."[36]

If a social worker had been on the call, which is what we're hearing proposed in the media, the situation could easily have turned violent—especially if they had walked in on the murder in progress. At that point, the officer would have been responsible to protect not only themselves but also the social worker and anyone else present at a time when they need to focus on dealing with a dangerous, mentally ill individual.

Whenever an officer responds to a "check the welfare" call, the situation could be dangerous, unpredictable, and potentially volatile. It could quickly escalate into a suicide or a homicide. The line between suicide and homicide is razor-thin. Cops never know what they are walking into. If a call turns into a homicide and a social worker is present, that person could end up being the victim.

Mental health issues could be ascribed to almost every criminal in society. Criminality itself could be interpreted as mental illness. That term is used frequently and carelessly thrown around.

On one particular call, we went to check on a man who hadn't been seen in a while. When I knocked on the front door, no one answered. I walked around to the back, found an open window, and climbed in. It was dusk, and the house was dark inside.

Let me tell you, that is scary. We have no idea what we are going to encounter. All too often, we find dead bodies on these welfare calls. (This is about to get very descriptive, so if you're sensitive to graphic images, you might want to skip the next paragraph.)

We were cautiously going through the house with our flashlights on. I went into a bedroom and saw the man's severed head sitting on a desk staring at me, with his decapitated body on the bed, positioned as if he were sitting up against the headboard.

It turns out he was killed by his son and left there.

I can't tell you how many bodies I have found on these welfare calls. This is one of the things cops rarely talk about in our profession—the constant exposure to this kind of activity. That image will never leave me. It remains a part of who I am now.

These encounters imprint on officers' souls and affect their mental health.

Suicides Are on the Rise

The number of officers facing post-traumatic stress injury (PTSI) is going through the roof. This "war on cops" is far more insidious than physical acts. It encompasses a political war that affects the morale of officers around the country.

Add these stressors of the current sociological issues facing law enforcement—politicians turning their backs, complacent media painting cops with a brush of racism, and the authority figures chosen by President Biden for top government positions spouting anti-cop sentiments.

Unfortunately, our country is seeing a startling amount of officer suicides, and that number is increasing drastically. In 2017, 129 officers died in the line of duty, but 140 died by suicide. Numbers released by Blue H.E.L.P. in January 2020 showed that 228 police officers took their own lives in 2019.[37]

Did you catch that?

More officers die from suicide than are killed in the line of duty.

This is heartbreaking. Many of the mental health issues facing cops come from the stress they see every single day on the streets where they witness horrible violence, deadly car crashes, and homicides. Exposure to violence, cruelty, and death on a continual basis takes a toll.

Police are called to these situations every single day. They are trained to handle them, to calm the situation down. Every day they deal with people who have mental health issues.

Suicide by Cop

Sometimes a call will lead to "suicide by cop." This is an unofficial term and happens quite frequently. A suicidal individual will deliberately cause a confrontation with an officer using a lethal weapon. Sometimes, they will pretend they have a gun and move in a way to create this illusion, such as putting their hand in their pants and pulling their hand out quickly, or pointing a finger or stick at a cop in a very low-light setting.

In that situation, the unarmed individual is killed by the police, who must shoot to defend themselves and keep others in the area safe. Sometimes, a misinterpretation of an action can lead to a death that should not have occurred. For instance, a suspect is shot because the police interpret that they have a weapon when in actuality, they don't.

Many of the people who commit suicide by cop don't have the courage to take their own lives, so they have someone else do it for them. This would be the definition of someone who is mentally ill, right? When this happens, it often becomes part of a narrative to paint that officer in a negative light.

Suicide is horrible, but suicide by cop leaves multiple victims: the individual initiating the encounter, the law enforcement officer, and the families involved. Even when the investigators rule the shooting as justifiable, a civil suit will usually follow and drag on for years. This seemingly never-ending experience often creates emotional traumas that affect the mental health of the officers and their families. Even if the legal machine completely exonerates them, the officers will often retire or simply resign due to the stress. Every cop lives with the knowledge that the most routine call could lead to the fateful encounter of "suicide by cop."

No One Could Have Prepared Me for This

Tony Rodarte Speaks:

When I went through the police academy, I wasn't taught or prepared for what I was going to see as a homicide cop. They gave us the tools to stay alive, and they gave us the tools to act quickly under pressure, but we didn't spend any time on the reality of the kinds of people and crimes we would encounter.

When I was actively in law enforcement, I did not get help. I did not talk to a counselor, my co-workers, or my family about the things I encountered in homicide. I had to compartmentalize it, leave it at work, and come home.

Many days I wondered if there was any humanity left. Of course there is, but I got caught up in the day-to-day of going from one homicide to the next to the next.

My wife encouraged me to get help, but I wasn't comfortable asking for it. I didn't know how to initiate that conversation with my agency. Hopefully, my unit would have been supportive if I had asked for help, but I wasn't sure of the response I would get, so I stayed silent.

As officers, we don't talk enough about what is going on inside. I saw some horrendous things during my career that were so violent and disturbing that I wouldn't want to share them with others because those images are burned into my mind, and I can't get rid of them.

The general public does not understand how violent our world is. Very bad people do very bad things, whether they are luring children through the internet, victimizing children and adults with violent acts, or child predators looking for young children.

It's out there. It's all around us. We desperately need law enforcement to maintain peace and order. Every day, I was around families experiencing the worst day of their life as they found out a loved one had died. I needed help to process all of it.

I chose not to talk to anyone, and that's what we need to change. When I did retire, I found an amazing therapist, and she helped me tremendously. She gave me the tools to process and move past all the thoughts and images that keep rolling around in my head. The weight of the world lifted off my shoulders.

When I retired in 2018, my wife and I started a nonprofit organization called The Compassion Alliance to pay for trauma therapy for men and women who need those services. Law enforcement suicides are far greater than the number of deaths that occur while in the line of duty. I experienced firsthand that officers need mental trauma services.

—Tony Rodarte,
founder of The Compassion Alliance
and retired homicide detective,
Maricopa County, Arizona

The Fallen Blue

> "It is not how these officers died that made them heroes, it is how they lived."

During National Police Week, tens of thousands of people descend upon the National Law Enforcement Memorial, deep in the metropolis of Washington, D.C. This monument stands as a silent sentinel along a tree-lined pathway.

Driving by, you might not notice it. It is rather unobtrusive. Dark granite walls face each other, divided by walkways covered by a canopy of beautiful green leaves during the spring. Carved on these walls are the names of every law enforcement officer in the history of our nation who sacrificed his or her life in the line of duty.

Wives, husbands, children, and other loved ones of these fallen heroes, as well as thousands of uniformed law enforcement officers, visit this somber place in the middle of May to honor the hundreds who gave their lives in service to their communities the previous year.

Some will stand and stare at the name of the man or woman they loved, memories flooding their hearts. Others will kneel with their heads bowed, weeping silently, the tears falling from their cheeks joining the tear-stained concrete where thousands have kneeled for decades filled with the sorrow of loss.

Solitary officers stand at attention in full dress uniform and gaze upon the names of their fallen partners. Raising a hand in slow salute, cheeks glistening from tears, they seem lost in their memories.

They lower their salute and move forward to gingerly touch the name of their partner with their fingertips in a silent goodbye. Watching as they turn to walk away in what appears to be a slow march is an incredibly moving experience.

Should you spend any significant time in this place, you will watch this tableau repeated hundreds of times. Each day during that special week, a growing number of photos will adorn the wall, along with ever-expanding mounds of flowers.

Late in the evenings, groups of men and women will gather around the name of their fallen comrade, telling stories about funny moments they shared or tales of their bravery when the final moment came. Bottles of whiskey will be uncorked and paper cups produced as they raise those cups in toasts to their friends.

To a bystander, these images might appear repetitive, but in actuality, each of these individuals is having a unique experience. All of us grieve in conjunction with our own particular memories of those we have loved or honored, so these moments belong only to us.

During these days, several ceremonies will take place. Speeches will be made by politicians and police leaders. Each engraved name will be revealed and honored.

Those who have traveled miles to be a part of these ceremonies may be startled by the unveiling of their loved one's name. Seeing that name carved in the granite alongside thousands of others brings a stark confrontation of the finality of this moment. The moment of the recognition of "forever."

At the entrance to this monument of honor, a powerful phrase welcomes all to this hallowed ground:

IN VALOR THERE IS HOPE

These words, taken from a quote by a Roman senator, are now seen by all who come to this place. They are noble words to honor noble deeds of sacrifice for the good of others. They are fitting words for this place and all that it represents.

Every American law enforcement officer who gave their life in "The Line of Duty" will be represented here. Sadly, countless new names will soon be carved into the granite alongside the thousands of other heroes, a symbol of the reality of policing.

Even though I'm no longer a cop, I've attended National Police Week in Washington, D.C., every year for the past 30 years, and a lot of memorable moments take place there. But one memory that will remain with me for the rest of my life happened the same year that I was working on writing this book.

Imagine 25,000 cops in full uniform along with their families pour onto the national mall at dusk as music plays. Approximately 40,000 people participate in the candlelight vigil, lighting their candles at the same time, and holding the candles aloft in ceremonial respect for those we were killed in the line of duty that year.

It's an amazing sight and profoundly emotional.

One of the highlights of police week is watching the Police Unity Tour, which has been an annual tradition for more than

20 years. Cops from all over the nation will get sponsors to help raise money for the memorial fund by riding their bicycles from New Jersey all the way to Washington, D.C.

As I stood there behind the barricade this year, watching hundreds of cops who were all in the same bike uniform, all riding in together at the appointed time, I noticed a family of police survivors. I could tell they were survivors by their matching shirts. Each one was imprinted with the end-of-watch date of their loved one.

One of the family members is a two-year-old child, maybe younger. He's standing there with his mom and the rest of the family as the bicycles are coming in, waving a little memorial flag. Thousands of people are clapping and high-fiving. It's a joyous occasion to see the ride culminate in everyone arriving together at the memorial.

All of a sudden, this little boy grabs onto my leg and starts hugging my leg with one arm and waving the flag with the other. Now, I've never been married and never had children, so I'm not used to this. As he's hugging my leg, his mom turns to me and says, "That's what he used to do with his dad. We put his name on this wall this year."

That was the most powerful moment of the entire week for me—a moment that will remain with me for the rest of my life. I wish I could talk about that moment with every American because, for me, that puts everything into perspective. This is what our memorial means. And this is the sacrifice of these men and women.

This is the legacy of policing and a testament to how powerful that legacy is.

SECTION 4

MAKE AMERICA SAFE AGAIN

"It's your reaction to adversity, not adversity itself, that determines how your life's story will develop."

—Dieter F. Uchtdorf

Fighting for Reform

The surge in violence across our great nation has been catastrophic, yet we are only now starting to see a glimmer of hope, a little pushback from the narrative. For example, the radical city council in Minneapolis attempted to dismantle the entire police department. They were supposed to reimagine something different, but no one was ever told what that would be. Thankfully, that plan was defeated, but in Austin, Texas, the defund the police movement is alive and well.

In places like Indianapolis, Indiana, where Nikki Sterling has been working tirelessly to bring reform to The Bail Project, we are starting to see some glimmers of hope.

After Nikki's son was killed by a criminal who should not have been out on the streets, Nikki began her mission to spread awareness about the charitable bail organizations that are aiding violent offenders by bailing them out of jail. Nikki and her husband quickly took action to see what could be done to change this.

Nikki's husband, Jim Sterling, knew a former senator, so they met with him to find out how to bring in a law to amend the current ones. She found out that a bill had been proposed in 2021 to regulate charitable bail organizations, but it wasn't passed.

"We asked this former senator what we could do to dust it off and get it put back in front of Indiana state legislators for 2022," Nikki said.

The senator told them the bill needed to get in front of a senator or a member of the House, so Nikki set up a meeting with a senator. Jim also reached out to some people he knew.

Nikki worked for the passage of a bill that would prevent charitable bail organizations from bailing out anyone charged with a violent crime or with a previous felony conviction. The bill would also impose a $2,000 bail bond cap on misdemeanors. This means that offenders with higher bail (because they are repeat offenders, considered dangerous, or have committed crimes against children) would not qualify for bail relief. She testified before both houses to promote these bills.

She said, "If I can prevent this from happening to another family, my life has been purposeful, and I will have carried out the legacy of my son, who was always there to help those in need."

The Senate introduced Bill 8, authored by Senator Aaron Freeman. The House of Representatives presented their version, which was House Bill 1300. Bill 8 was rolled into House Bill 1300 and passed both houses before Governor Holcomb signed it into law.

According to House Representative Peggy Mayfield, who authored House Bill 1300, the bill brings fairness to the bail system so that these charitable bail agencies have to follow the same highly regulated rules as other agencies offering bail posting.

At the time of this writing, House Bill 313, or Madelynn's Law, is in the process of going to the Kentucky Senate for approval. This bill aims to restrict bond groups from posting bonds that are $5,000 or more.[38] This law's name came about because of the death of teenager Madelynn Troutt, who was killed in a head-on car crash by a man on a "drugged-out crime spree" after he was bailed out by The Bail Project for other offenses. Her family hopes that this bill, if passed, will keep other families from experiencing similar trauma.

Had The Bail Project not posted a $5,000 bail for Michael Dewitt's release from jail[39] several days before Madelynn's death, she would not have experienced a head-on collision with him.[40] In January, he was arrested and charged with theft of a motor vehicle and possession of a controlled substance, and he was listed as a fugitive. In February, when The Bail Project posted his bond, his charges included receiving stolen property over $10,000 (he was driving another stolen car), assault of a probation officer, resisting arrest, disorderly conduct, and public intoxication.

An investigation found that he had more than ten arrests and a lengthy criminal record. According to a March 2021 news article, "This time, Dewitt was charged with murder and driving under the influence of controlled substances, as well as leaving the scene of an accident, receiving stolen property, possession of a firearm and handgun by a convicted felon, and car theft. He's being held on a $500,000 bond."[41]

Citizens have to step up and take action to fix this problem. Parents need to unite and call for justice. We must all become activists who are part of the solution by gathering information and educating ourselves. This is where the rubber meets the road.

Exposing Injustice Against Law Enforcement

Many private citizens and organizations are stepping up to help bring fairness and justice to public safety. The Law Enforcement Legal Defense Fund (LELDF) is one such organization. A national nonprofit 501(c)(3) that, according to their website, policedefense.org, has "helped dozens of officers get their names cleared of wrongful charges … [they] make sure that these officers get back to doing their jobs instead of sitting behind bars."

I interviewed Jason Johnson, president of LELDF, on April 11, 2022, to get his perspective on how we can work together to rescue 9-1-1. As an attorney with experience in policing, policing management, and policing accountability, Johnson now serves as an advocate for law enforcement and for individual police officers who are unfairly scrutinized and maligned.

The 30-year mission of LELDF is to support law enforcement officers who are wrongly accused of crimes related to their law enforcement duties. Both a charitable and an educational organization, its core roles are to raise money to pay the legal fees for these officers as well as advocate for the police officers and the law enforcement profession.

"We identify cases where the officer acted lawfully and within their training, and yet, even though they have done that, they are still being prosecuted," said Johnson. "We provide funding to aid in their defense. We pay for attorney fees, expert witness fees, jury consultation, and sometimes we are even able to provide some funds to pay to the officer's family as they are going through this arduous ordeal."

An example of a case where they are successfully standing behind these officers happened when deputies James Johnson and Zachary Camden engaged in a high-speed pursuit of Javier Ambler, a convicted criminal who was high on illegal drugs.[42]

After 22 minutes of dangerous high-speed pursuit, Ambler crashed his car. As the deputies tried to secure him with handcuffs, this 400-pound man had a heart attack and could not be revived with CPR.

Two years later, out of the blue, the newly elected district attorney in Austin, Texas, José Garza, charged deputies Johnson and Camden with manslaughter.

During our interview, Jason Johnson said, "Two officers who were doing their job pursuing a fleeing convicted criminal have had their careers ended and could face decades in prison. LELDF stands behind these officers and will do everything it can to provide the best defense possible for these heroes. These officers have put their lives on the line for us. As citizens, we must protect them when they are in the right."

The second mission of LELDF is to educate the public on the many challenges and dangers faced by law enforcement in their duties. They accomplish this through their website, social media, direct mail campaigns, and educational engagements.

"Sometimes we promote this education by giving public presentations, but oftentimes we do this by using our use-of-force simulator called Decision Points," says Johnson. "We can bring members of the public, the media, elected officials, and others into this simulator to experience firsthand what it is like for officers responding to dangerous, sometimes life-or-death situations."

The in-person simulator, located in the LELDF office in Washington, D.C., creates an immersive experience with filmed incidents. Participants are expected to interact with the screen as they would if they were a police officer, including using force, if necessary.

They have all of the tools that an officer would have, such as a real gun (unloaded, of course) and a taser. The room is equipped with a large movie screen, and sensors are placed around the room. The tools are all programmed to respond with lasers.

As the simulation begins, the participant has to make split-second decisions in high-stress situations. Afterward, we debrief with a professional police trainer who conducts the training as if the participant were an entry-level police recruit doing this for the very first time.

"One of the things that we've found that has been the most impactful," says Johnson, "is that people don't understand what happens to the human body when it's under stress. That's why it's so critical to be able to replicate, in some way, the stress that police officers feel when they respond to a life-and-death situation. When we are successful at doing that, they experience physiological changes. They get tunnel vision. They get auditory blockage. Their heart rate starts racing. They have a hard time reacting. They feel like their feet are stuck in sand.

"During the debrief, what they notice is that they can't remember very critical things. They completely forget things that happened 10 seconds ago. They can't answer questions like, 'What did this person say?' or 'What color shirt was the guy with the gun wearing?' They can't remember. That's a great teaching point because one of the things police are criticized for is for being unable to give a 100% perfectly accurate account of what happened in a situation. Or why what's shown on the body camera differs from what police officers on the scene remembered happened. It shows that they're not lying. It's a unique experience when you're under that kind of stress. Your body is focusing on only what it has to to survive the situation. Everything else just gets cast aside."

If you're interested in experiencing the online simulator for yourself, you can navigate to it from the LELDF website at:

policedefense.org/decisionpoints

From their website:

> **Decision Points** is an immersive experience designed to place participants "in the shoes of" a law enforcement officer responding to dangerous situations. Participants interact with the scenario by responding to periodic prompts, called "decision points." There will be initial, brief feedback on the appropriateness of the chosen action with more detailed information provided at the end by LELDF police practices expert, Sergeant William Gleason, at the end of the scenario.

> **About Sergeant Gleason**
>
> William Gleason is a veteran law enforcement officer and training instructor with over 30 years experience. He has trained thousands of law enforcement officers in firearms, defensive tactics, force de-escalation, and use-of-force assessment and tactics. Sergeant Gleason is certified by the Force Science Institute as a Force Science Analyst. He has testified as a police use-of-force and police practice expert in federal and state courts.

The online simulator is different from the in-person simulator in that you're in the comfort of your own home, you don't have an audience or feel like you're going to be critiqued, but you get to see everything from the perspective of the officer and make decisions about what to do in each scenario. You'll have much longer to make decisions during the simulation than you would in real life, but you can see how your decisions line up with how a trained officer should respond.

Getting a glimpse of what officers face on a daily basis is one of the keys to fighting for America's safety. When you know the truth, the truth will set you free. If each one of us will arm ourselves with the truth, together we can rescue 9-1-1.

The Wounded Blue

In 2021, a state police agency contacted me to ask for help in getting treatment for one of their officers who had been on the job for twenty-five years. This officer was in charge of the "shoot house," which houses a live-fire exercise where cops learn how to do building searches and shoot at targets. This real-life scenario is held inside a building, so over the years, the officer had been breathing in the lead from the shooting exercises.

His doctor diagnosed him with lead poisoning, but the worker's comp insurance company said they would not pay his bills. His request went all the way up to the commandant, who then called the worker's comp people. They replied that they didn't work for his department. They worked for the governor. They said this to the commandant of the state highway patrol. He couldn't get his officer's bills paid.

In another case, a lieutenant who was in pursuit of three hired killers got shot in the head. He wrecked his car doing over one hundred miles per hour.

His medical bills went unpaid for a year and a half. He lost his car, then his house. Finally, one day a news station did an exposé on the story, and suddenly his medical bills got paid. He also received a $35,000 severance and was asked to leave.

This is the reality of what's happening to law enforcement officers in America today. This corrupt system is destroying the lives of police officers, so our mission at The Wounded Blue is to be a voice for the voiceless. Every day, we declare war on a corrupt medical system and a broken worker's comp system—a big fight because large amounts of money are at stake for these insurance companies.

Making a Change by Changing the Language

Words hold power. The Wounded Blue works hard to change the vocabulary within the law enforcement community. Its mission revolves around the acronym S.E.A.L.—Support, Education, Assistance, Legislation.

We created a training program called "Walking with the Wounded." This course prepares the leadership in law enforcement to handle a situation where one of their officers is seriously injured in the line of duty. The goal is to alter the police culture to create a winning scenario when a department encounters these situations. This is where the use of words can be life changing.

When a police officer is accused of serious misconduct, they are put on administrative leave. When a police officer is involved in a shooting, most departments *also* put them on administrative leave, thus equating misconduct with the use of force, one of the most pivotal acts an officer must perform in the line of duty.

Labeling these the same way negatively impacts the officers and the public. Through "Walking with the Wounded," we teach the chiefs to put these officers on *critical incident leave*, not administrative leave.

This simple change in language and protocol can alter the officer's experience and alter our culture. If an officer is involved in a shooting, the correct term is a "critical incident," so it should be labeled as such.

Over the course of their career, a police officer's life might be made up of a series of these critical incidents. Any one of these could cause a post-traumatic stress injury.

Most of us know what PTSD stands for—post-traumatic stress disorder. However, in the law-enforcement world, The

Wounded Blue is working to change that definition to PTSI—post-traumatic stress injury. This is a more appropriate term when it comes to an officer handling an event in the line of duty. An injury can be fixed or treated. A disorder sends the connotation of being mentally ill. An injury does not always lead to a disorder. An injury can be treated.

Carefully choosing the words we use to describe situations can make a huge difference in how each situation is handled.

A Rundown Area of Atlanta Gets a Facelift

In Atlanta, a rundown apartment complex in an area riddled with crime got a new name and a facelift. Formerly called The Bluff, it is now known as Unity Place, and it is the first of its kind nationwide.

A few years ago, the city acquired the complex and turned it into one-to-four-bedroom units for police recruits to stay on a first-come basis during their weeks-long training program. Besides the apartments, which can house up to thirty officers, there is also a gym in the basement and an area for community meetings.

Atlanta Police Foundation President and CEO Dave Wilkinson said the city and developers have plans to build up to fifty houses for city officers. Wilkinson said the officers who move into these houses could receive up to a $500 monthly stipend by participating in community events.

This creates a win-win situation where the officers spend more time in the community getting to know the residents of their area, and the residents can get to know their law enforcement officers as part of the community.

According to *The Atlanta Journal-Constitution*, Thelma Reneau, a lifelong English Avenue resident and treasurer of the neighborhood association, said she's thrilled to see more officers in the community. "I'm gonna get to know them," said Reneau, 75. "I bake cakes, so I'm gonna bring them cakes and cupcakes."[43]

Recall Efforts Spark Positive Change

People around the country are waking up and becoming more active in their local politics. They have had enough of the rising crime in their cities and want to be proactive in changing the dynamics.

Let's not forget San Francisco residents who voted to recall the District Attorney, Chesa Boudin. Boudin was elected on an agenda of criminal justice reform but faced intensifying backlash from law enforcement, conservatives, and residents concerned about crime.[44]

Boudin had vowed, "… not to prosecute [so-called] 'victimless crimes' such as prostitution, open drug use, and drug dealing."[45] Since his half-term in office, San Francisco's crime rates have risen astronomically. Shoplifting, homelessness, and drug overdoses increased, along with reports of increased car break-ins, thefts, and burglaries.

Ballot measures, such as a recall, can be an effective way to fight back on well-defined issues. Public safety, justice, clean and protected neighborhoods, and stopping politicians from abusing power are too important to be ignored until the next election.

This recall happened after an already-successful recall of three school board members, Alison Collins, Gabriela Lopez, and

Faauuga Moliga, for prioritizing social justice politics over reopening schools and managing finances during the Covid lockdown.

Los Angeles DA Barely Survives Recall Effort

Likewise in Los Angeles, 97.9% of the 800 deputy district attorneys in Los Angeles County voted in support of an effort to recall their boss, District Attorney George Gascón.[46]

This group, the Association of Deputy District Attorneys (ADDA), invited Gascón to meet for a discussion about his policies and a proposed recall that could potentially take him out of office. He refused the invitation.

The president of the ADDA, Michele Hanisee, said, "Over a year ago, Gascón began a massive social experiment by redirecting prosecutorial resources away from enforcing the law while simultaneously ignoring large portions of the penal code. The result is an emboldened criminal element that knows the DA will not hold criminals accountable. This experiment needs to end."

This group joined millions in the Los Angeles area to promote the most effective recall campaign in Los Angeles's history. This is unprecedented in U.S. history and shows what can happen when people band together for a united cause. The effort failed only because a number of signatures were disqualified by the Los Angeles County committee.

Becoming more involved in your local government is key. By researching upcoming candidates to know their views and values, you can help put politicians into office who have the same values as you do.

Texas Is Waking Up

In Harris County, Texas, four incumbent democratic criminal district court judges were beaten by their opponents. One of those judges was Greg Glass, who made headlines in September 2021 when Houston police officer, William Jeffrey, was killed in the line of duty. The officer was serving a narcotics warrant to a suspect and was shot and killed in that encounter.

Court records show that Judge Glass had not denied bail to that suspect in a prior case, even though he was a twice-convicted felon, so he was allowed to go free on lower bail.[47]

Smaller Cities Struggle to Keep Up

As violent crimes soar, smaller cities struggle to increase the size of their police force. In Roanoke, Virginia, the police department reported a 400% increase in homicides in 2021. This happened after city leaders cut the police budget in 2020 following the death of George Floyd, and one-fifth of its force walked out.

The city eventually managed to approve a budget to increase officers' pay and hire more police to patrol the streets. But it takes time to fill those spots with qualified candidates, train them, and acquire the learning curve to become cops who excel.[48]

An Oasis in the Desert

In Pinal County, Arizona, Sheriff Mark Lamb, who calls himself "The American Sheriff," oversees and manages more than 650 employees. His department provides patrol support throughout the county, search and rescue, and specialized units from narcotics to an anti-smuggling team.

Sheriff Lamb is an old-school sheriff who believes in justice. He's not going to join any political movement that is anti-law enforcement. On his website, sherifflamb.com, he states that the department's focus is to lead by example, to continue to crack down on criminal activity with a focus on stopping drug flow into Pinal County, and to change the perception of law enforcement within their communities.

As a constitutional conservative, Sheriff Lamb has strong convictions about the country he serves. He believes in our republic and our constitution, he actively supports our second amendment rights, and he is determined to protect the rights and freedoms of the people in his county. Police officers from all over the country are taking note of his heroic leadership and are saying, "I want to work for this guy." He has to turn people away who want to join his team.

Pulling Back the Curtain on a Movement Based on Rhetoric

> *AUTHOR'S NOTE: This is an excerpt from the interview I conducted with Jason Johnson, President of the Law Enforcement Legal Defense Fund (LELDF) on April 11, 2022. Johnson retired at the rank of major after serving 25 years as a cop in Prince George's County, Maryland. Prior to joining LELDF, Johnson was the Deputy Police Commissioner of the Baltimore Police Department from 2016 to 2018. His work with the Decision Points simulator has been invaluable for helping to advocate for law enforcement, and he stays on top of data to shine light on the reality of policing.*

Jason Johnson Speaks:

One thing that has led us to this crisis of confidence in law enforcement has been a mismatch between the rhetoric where most people get their information (either social media or cable news) and reality.

We see an incredible difference between the way law enforcement is portrayed in those two venues and actual objective data. This is not about what I might think or what you might think about law enforcement—I'm talking about actual numbers.

For example, the use of force by police officers has never been lower. If you look at deadly force, the number of incidents in which police officers use deadly force has steadily gone down.

The largest agency started measuring these numbers in the early 70s. If you look at NYPD's numbers in the early 70s, the number of times police officers used deadly force was 800 to 900 times a year. Now it's like 20. It's been a steady, steady downward trend.

Accountability mechanisms for law enforcement have never been higher. Body-worn cameras, civilian review, the amount of training they receive—these things are in place, and it's not like they started yesterday. These things have been developing over time to professionalize law enforcement.

However, the perception from CNN or MSNBC or from almost any social media platform is misleading. This has led to people calling for change. Change has already happened. It is happening. It has been happening for decades.

We're actually in a really good place in policing in terms of professionalization, reducing unnecessary uses of force, trying to find less lethal alternatives, and emphasizing de-escalation. All those things are in a very good place. Anyone who studies the profession knows that, but those aren't the loudest voices you hear, and so many people have been led astray.

Polling that began at the beginning of the "defund-the-police" movement shows that people who live in the most crime-challenged communities don't want that. They never did want it. They want the police. Of course, they want professional police. They want police who treat the community well, who are well-trained and effective, but they don't want to defund the police.

They understand that reduced funding for police reduces training and reduces the number of police officers who are on their streets fighting crime. They don't want that.

To correct this, we must all start with valid facts about policing. We can have all the public discussions we want about policing (and we should), but, first, we all must agree upon certain facts. You can't start instituting solutions based on faulty information. That's what has happened so far.

In the subsequent years since the George Floyd case, we've seen a huge increase in violent crime. We've seen skyrocketing levels of homicides and nonfatal shootings, and those are focused mostly in urban centers and cities that are primarily Black and brown communities.

Leadership in cities, and even at the federal level, seem to be turning a blind eye to that. Although they say Black Lives Matter, what has flowed from these policies has impacted Black lives in a negative way more than anything remotely related to the actions of law enforcement.

Today, we're starting to see some indication of the proverbial pendulum swinging back in a more moderate direction. Many of the cities who initially defunded the police are now re-funding the police, or reauthorizing spending on law enforcement, and pushing to hire more police officers.

We're seeing efforts to recall some of those prosecutors who have been elected who aren't really prosecutors—the ones not interested in prosecuting or holding people accountable for crimes (unless they are police officers).

We are seeing early signs of a return to moderation. But I'm concerned, and I know many other people are concerned that it won't happen quickly enough.

—Jason Johnson, president of the
Law Enforcement Legal Defense Fund (LELDF)

Standardization Is Key to Success

The social justice movement has not been about positive change but about punishing the police with narrative rhetoric while defunding their departments. Instead of putting all their time and effort into destroying law enforcement, we could have made significant change.

This is where the federal government took a wrong turn. They are making claims about issues with policing but have done nothing positive to change them. We could have used the George Floyd incident to create better policing instead of punishing the police.

We need a wake-up call for police leadership. Instead of defunding the police, we need to re-fund them and create standardization for basic training. Let's make our cops better by training them. Let's change the culture and be sure they have the training that is crucial for effective policing.

The massive disinformation campaign around police reform is about revenge against the police, making them the villain. Policing doesn't need to be reformed. It needs to evolve and incorporate all the advancements that have taken place.

As a nation, if we genuinely want to revolutionize law enforcement for the better, we have the opportunity to do it, but change requires a substantial amount of money and a commitment by federal, state, and local governments with funding for training our police officers. Effective training is expensive, yet it's the single most important aspect of improving policing. We can make our officers better by giving them the tools to succeed.

After officers go through a police academy, they might never have to take a physical fitness test again. In addition, many departments might only mandate a few hours a year of in-service training. We expect the physician who operates on us to have many hours of continuing education throughout their career, yet we don't mandate this for such a crucial profession as law enforcement?

The U.S. has approximately 18,000 police agencies across the country, with about 80% having fewer than twenty officers. Each of these might have different recruitment policies, training programs, and different leadership.

In the area of recruitment, police agencies feel a lot of pressure to hire officers who are of the same ethnic group as the makeup of the community they serve. If a community is 40% African American or 40% Hispanic, the politicians demand that 40% of that department must be the same.

This means the hiring standards and requirements have to be lowered in order to meet these percentages. This lowers the effectiveness of the police department. I'm not saying standards have to be lowered because a certain ethnic group is inferior. I'm pointing out that finding candidates to fit a specific peg becomes the goal instead of hiring the best candidates who show up, regardless of their race or ethnicity.

This happened in Miami in the early 1980s when law enforcement agencies were required to fill a quota for Spanish-speaking cops. They had to keep lowering the standard to get enough cops to fill the quota. They lowered it to the point that if an applicant spoke Spanish, they could be hired. What happened? They hired drug dealers! Those drug dealers in uniform destroyed the reputation of the Miami-Dade Police Department.

Police agencies across the country have dealt with corruption issues. One of the common denominators is recruitment and the standards used to hire their people. We need to change this and standardize the requirements to become a police officer.

If we lower our standards, we create a self-fulfilling prophecy because many of the new hires shouldn't be wearing a badge. We need to make these requirements standardized, so we get the same quality of cop across state lines.

Giving Cops the Tools to Excel at Their Job

In the area of training, officers must be proficient in myriad skills, unlike most other professions. That is why policing is unique and cannot simply be taught in the classroom. Many of the skills are perishable, so police training is always a job in progress.

If you look at agencies across the country, you will see a massive gap in the way cops are trained. They have no consistency. Even the number of hours of basic training can vary across states. Every officer gets trained in the key areas, including criminal law, firearms, and de-escalation techniques, but the methodologies vary.

We need to look toward programs where all cops will have the same skill level across the country with required yearly retraining. Every state has Police Officer Standards and Training (P.O.S.T.) requirements, the rules and regulations for how much basic training an officer receives and how much annual training is required. Unfortunately, many agencies have reduced the number of hours of in-service needed to meet minimum state mandates. We can revolutionize policing by putting standard protocols in place.

Las Vegas is an example of a department that encourages more training and gives officers the opportunity to do it. They are the ninth-largest department in the country and are considered one of the best police departments, partly because of the training their officers receive. They have an entire training catalog of programs to advance an officer's expertise in a particular area, such as firearms or criminal investigation.

We need to have minimum training requirements for all officers in the U.S., and they need to be enforced. Many states have minimums, but they don't have the budget, or they don't enforce these requirements, so the officers don't get the training.

If we want to change our trust in our police, we need to give them the skills and abilities to do their jobs and get the best outcome. This way, a small agency in Alabama would get the same level of training as the officers in the Las Vegas Metro PD. With this high-quality basic training, we will have better policing everywhere.

When the police are "defunded," the budget for the cop cars and equipment don't get slashed. The training budget gets slashed. Years go by, and police officers are not able to hone their skills.

Mandating more training nationwide would be a start, but they also need the funding to carry through with the training. Many departments spend hundreds of thousands of dollars on the latest drone technology, but they won't spend thousands of dollars to invest in trainers to teach officers how to be competent in advanced skills.

By standardizing the annual training and skills, every officer will benefit. Maybe the requirements could be eight hours of firearms recertification, eight hours of criminal law recertification, and eight hours of de-escalation, or cultural awareness training. Whatever the standards, every police officer in the country would be required to complete them, including the funding for the training.

When I was with the Las Vegas police, I was in charge of advanced training for the department. I wrote an article called "Policing with Honor," which was widely published by police magazines and periodicals. The article was about how to survive your career ethically, as well as physically and emotionally.

That topic struck a chord. I had police agencies asking if I would present this for them, so I created a training program called "Policing with Honor," an eight-hour training course that I taught all over the country. I've trained thousands of officers to "police with honor."

Placing Value on Safety

Another area that needs to be addressed is pay and compensation for law enforcement officers. With no regulation for this across the board, every state is different. I know an officer who makes $9.82 an hour, putting his life on the line every day. That is less than someone flipping burgers at a McDonald's. Other officers I know are making $15 an hour. If we want quality people, we have to provide fair compensation to bring in those people.

The motivating factor in most officers' decision to become a cop is the desire to help others. Unfortunately, that often comes with the sacrifice of being in a profession that doesn't pay enough. Tons of officers in police agencies around the country make $35,000 a year. If a police officer has a family to feed, they can't do it on that salary. They have to take on an extra job or two—maybe a security guard at a Walmart store, directing traffic at a construction site, or any other part-time job to supplement their income.

These cops are working their 40-hour police job and then working 20 to 40 hours in another job. They are exhausted, overworked, and sleep-deprived. Making life-and-death decisions on the job while being severely fatigued is highly dangerous. To revolutionize policing, compensation needs to be consistent with a living wage in each state.

The cost of living is different around the country, so a sliding scale should be used, but the salaries need to be raised to a level where officers can thrive on their salary.

Consistent Medical Compensation for Officers Injured in the Line of Duty

Another area that needs to evolve is care for officers who are physically injured or disabled as well as services for post-traumatic stress injuries. We are losing our officers to post-traumatic stress injury at a level never seen before in history. We have a suicide rate that is off the charts.

Officers need consistent medical treatment for on-duty injuries, whether those injuries are physical or psychological. The tragic reality is that an officer injured or disabled in the line of duty receives different treatments between counties, cities, and states.

In New York City, if an officer gets injured and disabled, they will receive at least two-thirds of their pay, tax-free. Their medical bills will also be taken care of for the rest of their life.

Another officer in a different state could be shot in the head, permanently disabled, and fired the next day with no compensation. Most people don't realize the discrepancies that exist in this arena.

To sum it up, let's look at the list.

- Standardize recruitment
- Create a living wage that is consistent for policing across the country
- Standardize training, both in basic training (the police academy) and advanced training on an annual basis
- Standardize medical services and compensation for officers injured in the line of duty

If we can accomplish changes in these areas, we will see improved policing, which will benefit the whole country—every town, every city, every state. That's where we need to aim. Instead of defunding the police or reimagining them, we revolutionize the system. That's meaningful change.

Courage Takes Many Forms

Recently, two neighbors had a dispute in a rural area of Washington State. One neighbor was burning leaves in their backyard, and the smoke was blowing into his neighbor's yard. That neighbor, who was very intoxicated, asked his neighbor to put out the fire. The neighbor burning leaves refused. The drunk man went into his house, got his twelve-gauge shotgun, brought it outside, fired up in the air, and went back into his home.

The police were called, and two deputies arrived at the scene. At this point, the drunk man was looking at a misdemeanor crime for firing his weapon into the air. The police were deciding on a strategy to proceed when they were suddenly ambushed. The man in the house opened fire and hit both officers in the head.

The officers were both critically hurt. Luckily, the man had birdshot in the shotgun and was at a distance, but the birdshot still hit both officers in their faces and eyes, so they couldn't see.

These two officers were now in the most precarious position a police officer can imagine. They didn't have their vision. They were sitting ducks waiting for this individual to come out and kill them.

The neighbors intervened. One had an AR rifle, and another had a pistol. Together, they engaged with the suspect to create cover fire and safety for these officers. Meanwhile, a third neighbor led the officers to safety. Because of the bravery and willingness of these people to get involved, those officers were saved.

I visited with these officers in my role with The Wounded Blue. The fact that brave civilians saved them was a momentous occasion for them. They were incredibly humbled by this experience.

They both have a long road to recovery and will hopefully recover their eyesight, but the courage shown by these three ordinary citizens is a willingness in America to stand up for our police.

Courage takes many forms. This was a physical act of courage where they braved gunfire to help these deputies.

You also need courage to stand up for what you believe in and the courage to stand and vocalize your support for your law enforcement officers—especially when the culture is steeped in anti-public-safety rhetoric.

We need a concerted effort by you, your friends, your neighbors, and the citizens of this country to finally say, "Enough is enough." Vote people out who embrace this culture of criminality and hatred toward law enforcement. Vote people in who believe in public safety and the true meaning of justice.

Vote with your dollars. Find out which companies or individuals support the people in power who are anti-law enforcement. If you currently support these organizations by paying for their services or being a monthly subscriber, opt out. In this way, you can be part of a unifying group who, together, can cut off the money supply to those who are not supporting the people they represent.

Here are some other practical ways that you can help Rescue 9-1-1:

- The next time you see a cop, thank them for their service.
- If you love someone who serves in law enforcement, give them this book.

- Gift officers you know with Dr. Gilmartin's book *Emotional Survival for Law Enforcement*.
- Listen to *A Cop's Life* podcast at RandySuttonSpeaks.com and share episodes with people you think of while you're listening.
- Encourage officers who are struggling to reach out for help from The Wounded Blue.
- Engage with the online simulation exercises at policedefense.org/decisionpoints and encourage others to do the same.
- Contact the nonprofit Covering the Blue and volunteer to make Thin Blue Line blankets or donate toward shipping costs.
- Reach out to the Law Enforcement Legal Defense Fund (LELDF) and find out how you can best support their efforts.
- Make a tax-deductible donation to The Wounded Blue at thewoundedblue.org.
- Join **A Cop's Life**, a free online community for law enforcement to interact, find support, and share resources. Request membership at **acopslife.org**.

It's up to us as a community to take our heroes out of hiding and into the status of valor.

I ask the silent majority to break their silence and tell the world you support your law enforcement officers. This is the only way to bring about the change in this country that supports the public safety of us all.

AFTERWORD

NEVER FORGOTTEN, NEVER ALONE

"You cannot choose your destiny, but you can create your legacy."

—Lt. Randy Sutton (Ret.)

From Tragedy to Legacy

I've been a narcotics detective, a field training sergeant, a federal task force commander, an advanced training supervisor, and a certified police instructor. Before suffering a stroke in my patrol car in 2009, I achieved the rank of Lieutenant.

As devastating as the stroke was, I believe it gave me a great gift. The gift of clarity. With that clarity came a sense of mission. Since then, I've been exposed to a side of law enforcement that I didn't know existed: life after injury.

Right before the stroke, I was on patrol at 2:30 a.m. as the watch commander on "the strip" in Las Vegas. In this role, I would take a young patrol officer with me in my police vehicle to get to know the officers on my team.

We were sitting in the patrol car talking when I suddenly found myself talking slower and slower. I had no control over it. I knew right away that I was having a stroke. I stopped the police car and muttered to the best of my ability, "I'm having a stroke. Get me medical help."

I got out of the patrol car and started walking toward the passenger side. That's when I began speaking gibberish. Seconds later, I couldn't speak at all. I couldn't move. I just crumpled to the pavement.

I lay there helpless. I wasn't afraid to die, but I was scared that I might have to live like this. I was utterly helpless. Tourists were walking past, taking photos of me with their cellphones as I lay there on a dirty Las Vegas street. Then, the backup guys arrived and encircled me to keep me from the indignity of being photographed like that.

They got me to the hospital, and I found out that a blood clot had gone through my brain. Thankfully, it didn't do anywhere near the damage it could have, but it ended my police career.

And then the unthinkable happened—my own department turned its back on me. The police administration said, "We're not paying your medical bills." I was dumbfounded.

The law states that when an officer is injured on the job, the department is required to pay the medical bills. Still, they refused to pay. That's when I went to my private insurance company. They said they would not pay my bills either because it was a worker's comp injury.

So I had to get an attorney to take my department to court. I fought for a year to get them to follow the law. Rather than just paying my medical bills, they ended up paying tens of thousands of dollars in taxpayers' money to fight me. They knew they had to pay; they just didn't want to do it.

I won, but they abandoned me. They threw me away. I went to the sheriff and asked him how he could do that to me after all my years of service. I served with this guy for 24 years, and he looked me in the eyes and said, "Randy, this isn't personal. This is just business."

I found out what it felt like to be abandoned, to be alone. My mother had died in my arms three weeks before my stroke. I'd been involved in a fatal shooting two months before that. And now, I had lost my career. I lost everything that was my life.

I was floating around, helplessly trying to figure out what I was supposed to be doing. I started to think about my legacy. How was I going to be remembered?

Around that time, police officers from all over the country started contacting me with their horrific stories: Being shot in the line of duty and not having their chief visit them in the hospital. Suffering stab injuries and the department not paying their medical bills.

The stories kept coming in. Not one story or two, but these heartbreaking stories were piling up from all over the nation.

Everyone said the same thing: "I feel abandoned."

That's when The Wounded Blue was born. The motto we live by is: "Never Forgotten, Never Alone."

My entire team consists of officers who have been shot, stabbed, beaten, run over, screwed up, and screwed over. Yet, they still want to serve. I call that a warrior spirit. They are fighting against an unseen enemy. It can be debilitating, but it can also be incredibly heroic.

I found out that there was no national resource for these men and women. There is already a high suicide rate for police officers, and when you add a disabling injury, it goes up about a thousand times.

Through The Wounded Blue, we've helped thousands of officers in the last several years and have saved countless lives. All of this was born out of a moment of terrible loss for me. If I had not gone through what I thought was the worst experience of my life and the worst loss of my life, I would not now be in a position to touch the lives of others in this way.

I could never have imagined this path when working as a lieutenant—writing books, appearing on television shows, or landing roles in feature films. With a broken body, I entered into a broken system that still desperately needs repair.

As I encountered more and more officers in similar situations, I realized we all needed the same thing: emotional and physical support. I've dedicated my entire life—my retirement years—to travel all over the country supporting injured officers and to be a voice for law enforcement. It's not easy, but it's worth it.

I've also spent the last decade training thousands of law enforcement officers nationwide—police academy recruits, chiefs, and sheriffs—with my "Policing with Honor" seminar. Speaking from the heart and drawing from decades of experience, I explore the career of policing through concepts of kindness, courtesy, and compassion.

My hope is that any time you see a man or woman wearing a blue uniform, you see them through my eyes. Not the way they're being painted by the media. Not through a broken lens.

Rather, see those people who are going to work every day, risking their lives, as men and women of valor. They're people like you and me who grew up in a neighborhood like yours or mine. They're someone's son or daughter. Someone's brother or sister. Someone's mom or dad. Someone's aunt or uncle. Someone's cousin or friend.

They're someone you can call in your worst moment.

Someone you can trust to help you, whether you just experienced a drive-by shooting or you can't find your kid in the grocery store.

They've been trained to know what to do in an emergency.

They're the ones who get dispatched when you call 9-1-1.

They show great courage in the face of danger—on purpose—every day.

They are men and women of valor.

But they are being painted as the enemy.

The Fight for the Soul of America

We're supposed to be living in a civilized society, but that society is breaking down right in front of our very eyes.

The entire public safety aspect of this country, which we once viewed as a critical part of our civilization, has now been altered. And it is going to take our communities—Black, Caucasian, Latino—to band together. If we do that, we can see a nation that is stronger than ever before.

That's the whole purpose of this book: to bring truth to the American people who have been fed so many lies. We've been fed so many half-truths and innuendos. We've been subjected to propaganda by a complicit media and a political movement—a movement that instead of protecting the people is protecting the predators.

Apathy is the fertilizer in which the breakdown of society has grown.

As Americans, we either don't vote at all, or we tend to vote for the person who makes the most noise. Well, that person typically has the most money backing them, so the best-funded person wins.

That's why George Soros has been so effective in undermining the entire criminal justice system of our nation. He has unlimited money to sway voters to support the candidates he handpicks, who are committed to undermining the criminal justice system in America.

Now, what are we gonna do about it?

Here's what we have to do: We have to empower our citizens to work together.

Instead of dividing, we have to unite. If a country is unified, it can't be destroyed. A united America is a strong America. The police are the symbol of a unified America. If we remove or weaken that symbol, we weaken America. And if the police can't protect themselves, they can't protect you or your family.

So, first, get informed. Find unbiased sources of information and educate yourself about what's happening in our country. Seek out a variety of perspectives. Do your own research. Be curious and compassionate. Action begins with education.

Next, get involved. Become an activist within your community. Becoming an activist does not have to have a negative connotation. It means simply engaging in an active way to enact social change. It means researching candidates at the local level and voting for ones who uphold your values. You might consider volunteering to help with political campaigns or at least being vocal about your decisions.

As we unify and work together, we will change the course of history. This is the way we will find justice again. This is the way we will heal.

But it will not be an easy battle.

Powerful forces are working against that—some within our own government.

Many years ago, the term "Power to the People" became popular. Power to the people means taking control of your communities, taking control of your own safety. Out of that grew support for the criminal justice system. A system that is fair. A system that is apolitical. A system that exists only to serve.

Demand that your police departments be fully funded. Demand that the police are given the ability to police. Demand that prosecutors and district attorneys do what their oath told them to do—actively prosecute violent offenders. Demand accountability from your elected officials.

Rescuing 9-1-1 is a fight for the soul of America.

It's time for the silent majority to stand up. We cannot afford to remain silent.

It's time to get out there and fight with our voices. Fight with our votes. Fight with our dollars.

It's time that we band together.

And be silent no more.

ACKNOWLEDGMENTS

Publishing a book feels very much like giving birth, except more than two people are involved with producing a book. *Rescuing 9-1-1* is a work that would not have been possible had it not been for the contribution of many talented and dedicated people. My thanks go out to the many Law Enforcement professionals whose insight and knowledge were essential to bring truth and honesty to these pages.

Dave and Betsy Smith, world renowned Police Trainers of "The Winning Mind"; Matthew Dages; Jamie Borden, Founder of "Critical Incident Review"; Jason Johnson, Executive Director of the Law Enforcement Legal Defense Fund; and so many others whose names you will read in this book.

Having access to amazing people of insight and experience is only a part of the equation of creating a book. It takes artistry in the form of editing, layout, artwork, and organizing to take ideas and form them into an easy-to-read and entertaining manuscript. I was very fortunate that a close friend and master marketing dude, Peter Anthony (who, by the way, strong-armed me into writing this book) introduced me to my co-writer, Lori Lynn, whose amazing patience and editing talent, along with Mary Rembert and Kathy Haskins, brought the words to life, and a special thanks to Shanda Trofe for the beautiful look of the book.

A special thanks to Matt Bennett for his help and encouragement.

Finally, I need to thank Paulette M. for her endless encouragement, ideas. and support throughout the creative process.

ABOUT THE AUTHOR

Randy Sutton is a 34-year law enforcement veteran and nationally known media commentator on law enforcement issues.

Over the past 10 years, he has trained thousands of police officers across the U.S. with his "Policing with Honor" workshop.

In July 2024, he addressed the Republican National Convention shortly after the attempted assassination of former President Donald J. Trump.

He has been featured on *Fox & Friends* and *The One America News Network* and is the "Crime and Safety" on-air personality for KTNV TV Las Vegas.

He has also appeared on hundreds of radio shows across the nation, including *Patriot Radio*, *Malcolm Out Loud*, *The David Webb Show*, and others.

His articles have been published in *The New York Daily News*, Townhall.com, *The Daily Caller*, PoliceOne.com, *Law Officer Magazine, Police Magazine*, and more.

As an actor, he was one of the most featured officers on the popular television series *COPS*, which led to his being cast as a police officer in the Academy Award-winning film *Casino* with Robert De Niro and Sharon Stone.

Other film and television roles followed, including *Fools Rush In, Miss Congeniality 2, The Road Home, Clovers Movie, America's Most Wanted*, and a co-starring role opposite James Caan in the pilot episode of *Las Vegas*.

He has appeared in numerous commercials and is the producer of a swing/big band music CD with some original compositions. His vocals and musical talent are evidence of a strong background in musical theater.

Born and raised in Princeton, New Jersey, Randy graduated high school and joined the Princeton Borough Police Department at age 19, becoming one of the youngest police officers in the state.

He served the town for 10 years before joining the Las Vegas Metropolitan Police Department, where he served for almost 24 years and retired at the rank of Lieutenant. During his service, he distinguished himself as one of the most highly decorated officers in LVMPD history, having earned multiple Life-Saving awards, Exemplary Service awards, Community Service awards, and a Medal for Valor.

Recognized by President George H.W. Bush for his creation of a reading program for inner-city children, he was presented with a Presidential Points of Light Award.

In his quest to help officers, he founded The Wounded Blue: The National Assistance and Support Organization for Injured and Disabled Law Enforcement Officers. Now Randy travels all over the U.S. and speaks, raising awareness and support for the nonprofit.

His book *The Power of Legacy: Personal Heroes of America's Most Inspiring People* became an Amazon #1 bestseller. During his police career, Randy penned three books about his and his fellow officers' experiences. These are *True Blue: Police Stories by Those Who Have Lived Them, A Cop's Life,* and *True Blue: To Protect and Serve.*

To reach Randy Sutton online or …

- Listen to his weekly podcast *A Cop's Life*
- Book him to speak at your next event
- Watch his 2024 Republican National Convention (RNC) speech
- Check out his music
- Connect with The Wounded Blue
- Buy copies of his books to give as gifts to your loved ones

… simply head over to:

RandySuttonSpeaks.com

Join the Fight Against Injustice

Every week, The Wounded Blue receives nearly 100 calls from wounded officers who have been injured or disabled in the line of duty. Through the Peer Support Advocate Program, these officers get the emotional help they need to recover after a serious life-altering injury that can lead to PTSI and even suicide.

As we work together to de-stigmatize mental health among the law enforcement community, we are helping to ensure injured officers receive emergency assistance, emotional support, and life-saving help—24 hours a day.

But we can't do it without the support of advocates like you.

You can join the fight against injustice—which is ultimately the fight for America's safety—by making your voice heard, advocating for law enforcement, and showing your support for our nation's heroes in a myriad of ways.

If you happen to have a heart particularly toward those officers who have been wounded in the line of duty, and you want to show your support in a tangible way, consider making a tax-deductible donation to The Wounded Blue at:

thewoundedblue.org/donate

Our mission is to help restore our heroes in blue back to their rightful positions—as men and women of valor—and to remind them that they are "NEVER FORGOTTEN, NEVER ALONE."

Together, we have the power to ignite a spirit of unity among our communities, rescue 9-1-1, and restore America's safety.

REFERENCES

1 "Henry Louis Gates Arrest Controversy," Wikipedia (Wikimedia Foundation, April 14, 2022), https://en.wikipedia.org/wiki/Henry_Louis_Gates_arrest_controversy.

2 LELDF Report, "Justice For Sale: How George Soros Put Radical Prosecutors in Power," Scribd (Scribd, June 2022), https://www.scribd.com/document/577278421/Justice-for-Sale-LELDF-Report#fullscreen&from_embed.

3 Stephanie Pagones, "Here Are 10 Times Legal Gun Owners Recently Thwarted Crimes in Life-Threatening Situations," Fox News (FOX News Network, February 16, 2022), https://www.foxnews.com/us/shootings-legal-gun-owners-safety-life-threatening-crimes.

4 Emma Colton, "New Orleans Mom, Iraq War Vet Pulls Gun on Man Trying to Enter Her Car: 'Locked and Loaded'," Fox News (FOX News Network, February 15, 2022), https://www.foxnews.com/us/mom-air-force-veteran-pulls-gun-man-trying-to-get-in-car-son.

5 New York Post, "12-Year-Old Kills Home Intruder after 73-Year-Old Woman Shot during Robbery," Fox News (FOX News Network, February 15, 2021), https://www.foxnews.com/us/12-year-old-kills-home-intruder-after-73-year-old-woman-shot-during-robbery.

6 Megan Brenan, "Americans Remain Distrustful of Mass Media," Gallup.com (Gallup, May 20, 2022), https://news.gallup.com/poll/321116/americans-remain-distrustful-mass-media.aspx.

7 Rachel Sharp, "Patrick Lyoya's Father Says He Was 'Killed like an Animal' by Police Officer," The Independent (Independent Digital News and Media, April 15, 2022), https://www.independent.co.uk/news/

world/americas/patrick-lyoya-police-shooting-footage-b2058834.html?src=rss.

8 "Pleasant Hills Officer Hailed as Hero for Saving 9-Day-Old Baby's Life," Pittsburgh (CBS Pittsburgh, April 28, 2021), https://pittsburgh.cbslocal.com/2021/04/27/pleasant-hills-police-officer-saves-baby-girls-life/.

9 Jaclyn Peiser, "A Drunk Driver Was Headed toward a 10k Race, Police Say. A Trooper Used Her Patrol Car to Protect the Runners." The Washington Post (WP Company, March 9, 2022), https://www.washingtonpost.com/nation/2022/03/09/florida-highway-trooper-crash-drunk-driver-10k/.

10 Molly Burke and Molly Sullivan of *The Sacramento Bee*, "Video: Cop Saves Man in Wheelchair from Oncoming Train," Police1 (McClatchy-Tribune News Service, August 13, 2020), https://www.police1.com/patrol-video/articles/video-cop-saves-man-in-wheelchair-from-oncoming-train-kHzrVji6ccvcivHg/.

11 "Ind. Cop Helps Boy Run Lemonade Stand, Makes Donation," Police1, July 29, 2020, https://www.police1.com/police-heroes/articles/ind-cop-helps-boy-run-lemonade-stand-makes-donation-4q7d7x3d2IXet4y6/.

12 "Video: Ariz. Cops Rescue Man Trapped in Burning Car," Police1, March 31, 2021, https://www.police1.com/patrol-video/articles/video-ariz-cops-rescue-man-trapped-in-burning-car-LlhB5H45suCzQ6xd/.

13 "Work Force Survey June 2021," Police Executive Research Forum, June 2021, https://www.policeforum.org/workforcesurveyjune2021.

14 Law Officer, "Illinois Police Department Disbands Citing 'Criminal Justice Reform Bill' as Contributing Factor," Law Officer, March 21, 2022, https://www.lawofficer.com/illinois-police-department-disbands-citing-criminal-justice-reform-bill/.

15 Danielle Wallace, "Understaffed Portland Police Forced to Shutter Cold Case Unit, Deal 'Devastating' Blow for Families," Fox News (FOX News Network, May 1, 2022), https://www.foxnews.com/us/portland-police-shuts-down-cold-case-unit-homicides.

16 Vic Ryckaert, "Mom Wants the Bail Project Reined in after Her Son Was Gunned down in Indianapolis," WRTV (WRTV, December 17, 2021), https://www.wrtv.com/news/local-news/crime/

mom-wants-the-bail-project-reined-in-after-her-son-was-gunned-down-in-indianapolis.

17 Nikki Sterling, "Op-Ed: The Bail Project Can Bail Out Anyone, Regardless of the Charge. That Should End." The Des Moines Register (Indianapolis Star, January 5, 2022), https://www.desmoinesregister.com/story/opinion/2022/01/05/bail-project-needs-regulation-indiana-son-murder-out-bail/9087566002/.

18 Vic Ryckaert, "Indianapolis Gave $150k to Group That Bailed out Man Accused of Killing Girlfriend," WRTV Indianapolis, August 6, 2021, https://www.wrtv.com/news/local-news/crime/indianapolis-gave-100k-grant-to-non-profit-that-bailed-out-man-accused-of-killing-girlfriend.

19 "Recidivism Rates by State 2022," Recidivism Rates by State 2022 (World Population Review), accessed July 10, 2022, https://worldpopulationreview.com/state-rankings/recidivism-rates-by-state.

20 Joe Marino and Kenneth Garger, "Career Criminal Indicted on Murder Charge Freed without Bail by NYC Judge," New York Post (New York Post, March 11, 2022), https://nypost.com/2022/03/10/criminal-indicted-on-murder-charge-freed-without-bail-by-nyc-judge/.

21 Morgan Rynor, "District Attorneys on Crime Rates: 'A Very, Very Dangerous Time Right Now in California'," abc10.com, December 1, 2021, https://www.abc10.com/article/news/politics/district-attorneys-crime-rates/103-165c64b4-49c6-471e-b407-947fa9ed5fbe.

22 Lawrence Richard, "California smash-and-grab at Macy's occurs at same mall where dozens of looters robbed Nordstrom last year," foxnews.com, June 19, 2022, https://www.foxnews.com/us/california-smash-grab-theft-walnut-creek-macys-nordstrom-crime.

23 Kenneth Garger, "Man Accused of Double Murder Less than a Week after Being Freed without Bail," New York Post (New York Post, November 4, 2021), https://nypost.com/2021/11/04/ny-man-luis-gabriel-ramos-accused-of-double-murder-less-than-a-week-after-being-freed-without-bail/.

24 Anthony Kuipers, "Police: Revised Reform Laws Provide More Clarity," Yahoo! News (Moscow-Pullman Daily News, Moscow, Idaho, March 11, 2022), https://www.yahoo.com/news/police-revised-reform-laws-more-141200603.html?.

25. Lorena Mongelli, "Long Island Judge Ignores Bail Law, Refuses Release of 'Menace to Society'," New York Post (New York Post, January 29, 2020), https://nypost.com/2020/01/28/long-island-judge-ignores-bail-law-refuses-release-of-menace-to-society/.

26. Joel B. Pollak, "Report: U.S. Has 75 'Soros-Backed' Radical Prosecutors," Breitbart, June 8, 2022, https://www.breitbart.com/politics/2022/06/08/report-u-s-has-75-soros-backed-radical-prosecutors/.

27. "District Attorney George Gascon's Flip-Flop Indicates a Fundamental Lack of Awareness by Samuel Dordulian, Esq..," Dordulian Law Group, December 21, 2020, https://www.dlawgroup.com/gascons-flip-flop-indicates-fundamental-lack-awareness/.

28. Alyssa Guzman for Dailymail.Com, "Woke St. Louis DA Refuses to Charge Armed Robbery Suspect Who Tried to Carjack Marked Police Car," Daily Mail Online (Associated Newspapers, March 22, 2022), https://www.dailymail.co.uk/news/article-10639633/Woke-St-Louis-DA-REFUSES-charge-armed-robbery-suspect-tried-CAR-JACK-marked-police-car.html.

29. Tom Hogan, "Manhattan's Likely New District Attorney Has Some Truly Radical Pro-Crime Ideas," New York Post (New York Post, July 6, 2021), https://nypost.com/2021/07/05/manhattans-likely-new-da-has-some-radical-pro-crime-ideas/.

30. Danielle Wallace, "Portland's police riot squad resigns after officer indicted over alleged assault on photographer," Fox News (Fox & Friends), June 18, 2021, https://www.foxnews.com/us/portland-police-riot-team-resigns-officer-indicted-assault.

31. Paul J. Weber and Jake Bleiberg Acacia Coronado, "19 Cops Indicted by Soros-Backed Texas DA Placed on Leave," Newsmax (Newsmax Media, Inc. Newsmax Media, Inc., February 19, 2022), https://www.newsmax.com/newsfront/texas-austin-jose-garza-police/2022/02/19/id/1057593/.

32. Chris Donaldson, staff writer. "Amazon Moves 1,800 Employees out of Downtown Seattle as Dangerous City Rages out of Control," BizPac Review, March 16, 2022, https://www.bizpacreview.com/2022/03/15/amazon-moves-1800-employees-out-of-downtown-seattle-as-dangerous-city-rages-out-of-control-1212819/.

33. Go Law Enforcement, "All You Need to Know About Police Background Check and the Common Disqualifiers," Copyright 2022,

accessed July 10, 2022, https://golawenforcement.com/articles/need-know-police-background-check-common-disqualifiers/.

34 Edwards, Lee. "Socialism: A Clear and Present Danger." The Heritage Foundation, October 11, 2019. https://www.heritage.org/progressivism/commentary/socialism-clear-and-present-danger.

35 Shubham Ghosh, "What is the 1033 Program? How the militarization of police forces has changed landscape of weapons on streets," MEAWW.com, Updated Sept. 9, 2020, https://meaww.com/1033-program-militarization-us-police-forces-landscape-law-enforcement.

36 Rachel Quigley, "Randolph Maidens: Unemployed Husband Who 'Murdered His Doctor Wife' Allowed to Return to Country Club Home," Daily Mail Online, Associated Newspapers, July 23, 2013, https://www.dailymail.co.uk/news/article-2375182/Randolph-Maidens-Unemployed-husband-murdered-doctor-wife-allowed-return-country-club-home.html.

37 Emerson Lehmann, "Study: Police More Likely to Die by Suicide than in Line of Duty," https://www.wsaw.com, accessed July 10, 2022, https://www.wsaw.com/2020/07/23/study-police-more-likely-to-die-by-suicide-than-in-line-of-duty/.

38 Natalia Martinez, "The Bail Project Previously behind One of Many Bonds for Suspected Killer Now on the Run," https://www.wave3.com (WAVE 3 News, January 2022), https://www.wave3.com/2022/03/02/bail-project-previously-behind-one-many-bonds-suspected-killer-now-run/.

39 Dennis Ting, "'It's a Tragedy': The Bail Project Responds to Deadly Crash Caused by Man Helped by Nonprofit," whas11.com, March 3, 2021, https://www.whas11.com/article/news/local/bail-project-dixie-highway-michael-dewitt-crash/417-e13c52e2-ebd3-40e0-b034-354d075bf56f.

40 Natalia Martinez, "The Bail Project Once Paid $5,000 Bond for Suspect in Wrong-Way Crash That Killed High School Cheerleader," https://www.wave3.com (WAVE 3 News, 2021), https://www.wave3.com/2021/03/02/bail-project-once-paid-bond-suspect-wrong-way-crash-that-killed-high-school-cheerleader/.

41 Heather Fountaine, "Man Charged with Murder in Dixie Highway Crash That Killed 17-Year-Old Girl," whas11.com (WHAS 11, March 2, 2021), https://www.whas11.com/article/news/crime/

madelynn-troutt-dixie-highway-fatal-michael-dewitt-murder-dui-charges/417-97651242-fcef-4e70-a5cc-9397df057e90.

42. "Deputy James Johnson and Deputy Zachary Camden—Williamson County, TX Sheriff's Department," LELDF, December 8, 2021, https://www.policedefense.org/deputy-james-johnson-and-deputy-zachary-camden-williamson-county-tx-sheriffs-department/.

43. Wilborn P. Nobles III, "Atlanta Opens New Apartment Complex for Police Recruits," Police1 (The Atlanta Journal-Constitution, February 7, 2022), https://www.police1.com/police-recruiting/articles/atlanta-opens-new-apartment-complex-for-police-recruits-wBSkZEKjU2byrRtk/.

44. Sam Levin, "San Francisco Recalls DA Chesa Boudin in Blow to Criminal Justice Reform," The Guardian (Guardian News and Media, June 8, 2022), https://www.theguardian.com/us-news/2022/jun/07/san-francisco-vote-chesa-boudin-recall.

45. Ryan Mills, "Majority of San Francisco Voters Back Recall of Progressive DA Chesa Boudin," National Review (National Review, March 16, 2022), https://www.nationalreview.com/news/majority-of-san-francisco-voters-back-recall-of-progressive-da-chesa-boudin/.

46. Christina Calloway, "L.A. County District Attorneys Association 'Overwhelmingly' Backs Gascón Recall Effort," MSN, February 22, 2022, https://www.msn.com/en-us/news/us/la-county-district-attorneys-association-overwhelmingly-backs-gasc%C3%B3n-recall-effort/ar-AAUb56L.

47. Mycah Hatfield, "10 Democratic Judges Lost Primary Election; 1 Heads to Runoff," ABC13 Houston (KTRK-TV, March 3, 2022), https://abc13.com/democratic-district-court-judges-harris-county-votes-chuck-silverman-abigail-anastasio/11615374/.

48. Emma Colton, "As Defund the Police Movement Trickles down from Big Cities, Small-Town America Pays the Price," Fox News (FOX News Network, August 3, 2021), https://www.foxnews.com/us/defund-the-police-movement-smaller-cities-increase-force.

STAY CONNECTED

A Cop's Life is a free online community where our everyday heroes—and those who champion them—can come together to interact, support each other, and share resources.

If you or someone you love is in law enforcement, it's important to remember that you've got a special calling on your life—and you are not alone.

Behind every badge is a heart that beats for our nation's safety. Connect with your sisters and brothers in uniform by going to:

acopslife.org

www.ingramcontent.com/pod-product-compliance
Lightning Source LLC
Chambersburg PA
CBHW070627030426
42337CB00020B/3935